Smart Mom's
Baby-sitting Co-op Handbook

How we solved the baby-sitter puzzle.

by Gary Myers

Printed in Canada

First Edition

ISBN 0-9678748-0-7

Editor: Peggy King Anderson
Book Layout and Design: Donna Jean Raines
Publishing Consultant: Val Dumond
Marketing Consultant: Kathleen Martin
Photography: Rodgers Photography
Cover: Linda Anderson

With my greatest admiration, this book is dedicated in memory of my ever-understanding mother, and my humble and courageous father. After all my mistakes, they assured me that I possessed better judgment; in my decisions they advised me to do what I thought best; and in their example, they were the kindest and most hospitable people I have ever known.

Contents

continued...

• Smart Mom's Co. Registration of Participation
• Authorization for Medical Treatment Form
• Smart Mom's Co. Order Form

Acknowledgments

Judy Manza has a surprisingly crisp mind for being a mother of five. Judy provided help in delivering a balanced presentation of the material in this book. Unable to find a free hour in Judy's schedule, I began to beg…. She relented and arranged a meeting at the local Laundromat. We did business between loads. Judy Manza is a long-time participant of the University Place Baby-sitting Co-op and has provided valuable insight into the secrets of what makes the Co-op so special.

I also want to thank all the participants of the University Place Baby-sitting Co-op for encouraging me to tell their story. They are an amazing group of talented women who have discovered a simple way to make their lives easier.

I also am grateful to Charlotte Klicker, my sister Linda Gilroy, Vickie Frick and Sid Morrow for their fresh perspectives.

Special thanks to my wife Patty for not giving up on me, for the quilt you made, and the buttons you still might sew.

Thank you all. I look forward to our next project…

Foreword

The University Place Baby-sitting Co-op changed my life. Before I joined the Co-op, I was locked into a 24-hour schedule. With three kids ages one, two, and five, I was overwhelmed. My relatives were hours from my home and I did not want to impose on friends and neighbors. I expected to manage everything myself.

I worked hard for my family. In five short years my active life had become a life of complete selflessness. I was there for my kids every minute of every day. When my shopping tantrums became worse than those of my kids, I knew I was on empty. I was not behaving like the mom I wanted to be for my children.

The Co-op gave me back the time I needed. I had a way to reduce my stress. I could help with kindergarten class or take my two-year-old to the doctor without the baby. Imagine my relief at knowing that I had a sitter every time I wanted! I was able to do more for myself and more for my children. Sometimes the smallest difference makes all the difference in the world.

I enjoyed getting out and I enjoyed having kids over. Through the baby-sitting Co-op, I met some wonderful people who will remain my close friends forever. I always love inviting new moms to be a part of our Baby-sitting Co-op. It is also my pleasure to invite you to take a close look at how a baby-sitting Co-op could give you the time you want and need.

Do this for yourself. Do this for your family. Do this to lend support to other moms. You will not be disappointed!

Patty Myers
Mother of three

"The credit belongs to those who are actually in the arena, who strive valiantly, who know the great enthusiasms, the great devotions, and spend themselves in a worthy cause; who at their best know the triumph of high achievement; and who, at their worst, if they fail, fail while daring greatly..."

—Theodore Roosevelt

Smart Mom's Quick Reference

- I want a quick summary of what this is all about—Go to Chapter 1.

- I just joined a friend's Baby-sitting Co-op and bought this book—Go to Chapters 8, 9 and Appendix A.

- I know of a large group of moms that may be interested in doing a Baby-sitting Co-op—Go to Chapter 6.

- I want to see the nuts and bolts of day-to-day paperwork—Go to Appendix A. Also review the Leader and Secretary Workbook forms. These can be downloaded from our free web site. For the web site address, call 1-888-974-2667.

- I want to jump in and start-up my own Co-op right now—Go to Chapter 4.

- I want to read how a Baby-sitting Co-op helps moms and strengthens the family—See Chapters 2, 7, 11, 12).

1

What Is a Co-op and Why Do I Need One?

Chapter 1

The Least You Need to Know (Questions and Answers)

What is a Baby-sitting Co-op?

It's a group of moms that agree to trade baby-sitting hours on a point basis. The cooperating moms take turns leading a few meetings and serving as Secretary to provide the simple bookkeeping needed. It is a long time between turns.

How does it work?

You can use your Baby-sitting Co-op as much as you want, or as little as you want. It's always a fair trade. You get out of it what you put into it. When you request a sitter, you spend points. When you sit for another mom, you earn points. Don't worry about points! Just make a deal with yourself to call for a sitter whenever you want. The points will work out—the secretary keeps track of everything for you.

What is the Smart Mom's Co-op Handbook for?

This Handbook will show the reader what a Baby-sitting Co-op is, how it works, and what to expect.

This Smart Mom's Baby-sitting Co-op Handbook is a rule book for being a participant in an existing Baby-sitting Co-op. The Handbook is also the instruction book for those who are thinking about starting a new Co-op with a few other moms.

A Smart Mom's Baby-sitting Co-op is designed to be started by any mom and three friends, or by any program director that serves a group of moms who have preschoolers.

Look inside this Smart Mom's Co-op Handbook to discover how the Co-op can work for you. Baby-sitting coverage will adapt to your needs and your schedule—not the other way around. See for yourself how easy it is to do a Co-op from scratch.

Where did this Baby-sitting Co-op Idea come from?

The Smart Mom's Baby-sitting Co-op system is based on the University Place Baby-sitting Co-op near Seattle, Washington. The University Place Co-op has been passed from mom to mom for nearly 20 years. Dozens of moms have participated in the Co-op over the years. The original University Place Baby-sitting Co-op was started by Mary Chapman, Judy Phillups, Teresa Christenson and a few others in the early 1980's. The University Place Baby-sitting Co-op continues today with new moms replacing the moms whose children have grown-up.

How many moms does it take?

A home-based Co-op can be any size. Most Co-ops start with just four moms. Some groups like to start recruiting immediately, other groups are happy to limit it to a few close friends until another good mom happens to cross someone's path. The most important thing is to be comfortable with those who will be watching your children. After awhile, moms usually see the advantage of having a few more moms. The idea is to get enough moms so that someone is always available. Home based Co-ops become too big with more than 20 moms. With fewer than 10 moms, Co-ops may eventually sputter to a stop.

A Co-op can also work for a large group or church. A large group can have one big Co-op or lots of small Co-ops. See Chapter 6 for start-up tips for large groups.

What do I need to do this?

Each participant needs a Co-op Handbook and each Co-op group needs the Leader Workbook and the Secretary Workbook. Workbooks can be downloaded free from our web site or purchased from the publisher. If you follow the steps, four Co-op handbooks are needed for the four moms who do the start-up. Call 1-888-974-2667 for the web site address.

How much does it cost?

Participants pay 12 dollars each September—that's all. Sanity is a bargain at any price—especially at only one dollar per month! The fee is for get-well cards, stamps, envelopes, cookies, and registration. The baby-sitting trades are free. Each participant must buy her own Co-op Handbook.

What about doing my turn?

The Co-op is designed to thrive without you. No need for extra work. No pleas for help. No guilt. Each participant serves a turn as Co-op Secretary or Co-op Leader. When you're done with your turn— you're done. Learn to let go. Move on. The Secretary's term is one month. The Leader's term is six months. Depending

Smart Mom's Shopping List for Start-up

- ❏ Four Co-op Handbooks
- ❏ One Leader Workbook and One Secretary Workbook
- ❏ Two 3-ring binders
- ❏ One pencil pouch

on the size of your group, you will be Leader once every seven years and Secretary once every year or two and you earn points for these jobs.

When it's your turn, you will be given the workbook that goes with the job. The paperwork is well organized. The workbooks have everything you need. This Co-op Handbook explains what to do.

What about the meetings?

The six meetings a year are a good excuse for a night out with other moms. Meetings have just the right amount of formality to keep things running smoothly. Moms enjoy bringing a touch of professional- ism into their work-lives. Volunteers host the meetings at home to earn extra points. If a large group starts a Co-op, Co-op business can be tacked-on to the end of the groups' existing meetings.

How does do I ask for time-out?

You make one call to the Co-op Secretary. She finds one of your friends (not a stranger) to sit for you. She takes care of all the details and the paperwork. No more hunting for a sitter. No more uncomfortable rejections. No more begging. The Co-op provides business-like customer service!

What is it like to be a sitter?

If you have ever volunteered to watch a friend's kids at your home, you already know what to expect. Since there will be lots of moms in your Co-op, someone will always be available to do a sit. This allows you considerable flexibility to do baby-sitting at a time when it works for you.

With the Co-op, best friends can be more than just a baby sitter. Call a Co-op sitter so you can take your best friend to lunch or go shop- ping together.

Why so many pages?

The rule-book for golf is hundreds of pages but the idea of the game is very simple. It is the same for the Smart Mom's Baby-sitting Co-op. The moms of the University Place Baby-sitting Co-op can teach a new participant all there is to know in just a few minutes. As for the Co-op Handbook, just keep it handy for easy reference. Most of the answers are in here.

> Be sure to read Chapter 2, to learn about the
> real-life benefits of a Baby-sitting Co-op.

Should I shop for another type of Baby-sitting Co-op?

There are two types of Baby-sitting Co-ops: Co-ops that use a Secretary to coordinate sits (centralized operation), and Co-ops that coordinate sits participant-to-participant (decentralized operation).

Co-ops that do not have a Secretary use tokens such as poker chips or playing cards to keep track of points. Both methods have advantages and disadvantages. Both types of Baby–sitting Co-ops have worked successfully.

The Smart Mom's Baby-sitting Co-op is designed to utilize a Secretary to coordinate sits. This centralized Co-op system can loosen rules so that sits can be arranged between participants. This allows the Co-op to enjoy the stability and hands-on management of the centralized Co-op, without loosing the ability to meet the needs of the participants. A Smart Mom's Baby-sitting Co-op is designed to provide a good balance. With a little flexibility, a Co-op having a Secretary will achieve the benefits of both systems.

Smart Mom's At a Glance

Will a Co-op Fit My Needs?

The purpose of the Baby-sitting Co-op is to help mothers of preschoolers have time out so they can better care for themselves, their families, and each other.

- Overworked? Need a break from the kids? Want to find some handy playmates? Do a Baby-sitting Co-op!

- A Co-op helps arrange free baby-sitting trades for a group of friends. It is not about teenage baby-sitters.

- A Co-op is for at-home baby-sitting. It is not about looking after a dozen kids. It's not about full-time child-care needs.

- A Co-op means less work not more. Extra work is not needed. Jobs rotate. Tasks are well organized. It is a long time between turns—and meetings. The Co-op is out-of-sight and out-of-mind most of the time.

- You can make yourself available to be a sitter at your convenience. You will not be locked into a fixed schedule of baby-sitting.

- The Co-op provides one call customer service. "We promise free time whenever you want it. No more hunting and begging for a sitter. It works. You can depend on it. And the sitter must be a trusted friend."

- Co-op start-up will be finalized after one meeting. Invite three moms over for an hour to do the *Eight Steps to Start-up*—it's that <u>easy</u>. Then get the word out. Moms will be knocking down the door to start. As the first Co-op Leader, you can expect a total time commitment of 12 hours spread over six months.

Comparison of Two Types of Co-ops

Centralized Co-ops with a Secretary

a. The Secretary finds the sitter—convenient customer service.

b. No fear of rejection when calling for a sitter—Secretary does the job.

c. Point system—Secretary logs points.

d. Secretary can monitor sit activity—useful to know who is available.

e. Participants tend to exchange sits with more moms—greater sense of community.

f. Greater depth of coverage when you need a sitter.

g. Easier to join—you get to know more sitters.

h. Can loosen rules—moms can arrange a sit together, then report it to the Secretary.

i. Tend to be more formal and have more stable structure.

j. Centralized leadership duty tends to bring out desire to preserve the Co-op and pass it on to the next generation.

Decentralized Co-ops Without a Secretary

a. Participants find their own sitter.

b. Participants may be reluctant to persist after rejections.

c. Able to select who you want to sit.

d. No Secretary on duty, track points with tokens.

e. It is more difficult to monitor sit activity—harder to see problems.

f. Participants tend to use the same sitters—smaller circles of support.

g. Less depth of coverage when you need a sitter.

h. New Participants must do cold-calls to find a sitter.

Chapter 2

Famous Last Words: "But I already have a few sitters."

"We fool ourselves into thinking we can manage but what really happens is we give up. We become housebound. How many of us always call one or two friends at the last minute? What happens when they say no? We have a choice. We either take the children with us and go crazy or cancel our plans."
    —Terry Highsmith, mother of three

This may come as a shock to you, but that static you hear on the phone when you call that special friend to baby-sit for the hundredth time is really a piece of paper being crinkled over the mouth piece—it is not a bad connection. Grandma, though she loves them dearly, gets tired too. She may say yes but she is really convinced you are only one tantrum away from a nervous breakdown. She is on a mission to save you from disaster.

Most moms feel it is not cool to ask friends or relatives to watch their children while they do something like read a book at the coffee shop. But sometimes that is exactly what a mom needs. That is why a Baby-sitting Co-op is different. You can get a sitter for any reason— and a sitter will always be available.

Life is stressful enough without having to juggle a dozen things and still worry about finding a sitter. The pressure on a new family is enormous—almost too much to withstand. Couples struggle to find time for each other while confronted with some of the most stressful challenges to face a family—finding a job, going to school, financial pressures, moving away from life-long friends. The list is endless—not to mention the sacrifices necessary to care for small children and adjust to a young marriage.

Young children need constant attention. That's a given. It's a tough job, one that should draw the highest pay in the land—forming the early years of a child's life, developing the attitudes and habits of young children, molding small minds into curiosity shops. But stress adds up. Even the simple things can become frustrating:

What parent hasn't mouthed these words during their children's pre-school years:

"Why can't I go to the bathroom without my kids knocking on the door?"

"Shopping for groceries has become the hassle that I hate most."

"Every time I get on the telephone my child develops a crisis."

"Oh for a few hours to treat myself to doing something just for me!"

The parent of a preschooler is often subjected to endless hours of children's babble, children's problems, and children's energy. To become effective parents, most understand the need to "take a break," get out and do something completely different, talk to grown-ups for a change, enjoy a few peaceful moments.

Moms need a break from the tie-down effect of caring for small children. Moms need a trusted friend, another loving mom, to step in and care for the children.

Moms trade lots more baby-sitting after joining a Co-op. For each baby-sitting trade, moms achieve a small victory over the daily stress. Moms solve problems, get things done, and take care of the family. Maybe this means an argument is replaced with a smile, a kind work substituted for an icy demand.

Little by little, day by day, the family is made stronger. Perhaps these tiny victories will bring one less divorce. Perhaps these will forever strengthen one more family. The small victories begin to add up—a little calm here, a little relief there. As each tiny stress is conquered, a mom makes a new place in her home for peace to enter. With a little time out, a mom has a bit more strength to bring a special touch to each room and to each child. With new found energy a mom gathers up peaceful things and thoughtfully arranges these in her home like colorful flowers carefully placed in a beautiful vase.

It is hard to believe something as simple as a Baby-sitting Co-op can make such a welcome difference. The fact is, without a solution, moms resign themselves to work harder and persevere more. The tie-down effect is viewed as just part of the job. This super-mom super-denial thing has driven more than one mom to a tearful reality-check.

Two things are certain—all moms need help sometime, and no matter how good your network, friends and family need a break too. A little more coverage, a few more friends to rely on, the joy of offering these solutions to another mom—it all adds up. A baby-sitting Co-op is a worthy place to find peace-of-mind and to share the same blessing with others.

True Stories

Most moms go through a period of trying to be super-moms. The Co-op moms at University Place clearly recall the moments that they decided it was time to look for help.

"I remember trying to take all three of my children to the doctor's office," says Julie Happenstall, mother of three. "The baby was in for a checkup and I was watching so he wouldn't roll off the patient bed when my other child started playing with an electrical outlet. The third stood up on a counter to reach for some stickers. The doctor walked in just as I was doing my special whisper-yell. Right then I knew it was time to join a Co-op."

Alice Watts considered herself "kind of a recluse" after the birth of her third child. "I took all three to church where my husband played the piano. The baby was nursing, the second child was very clingy and the third refused to go to classes. I had to take them into the hall where one of them proceeded to throw a tantrum. A crying baby, a child pulling at my dress and another screaming. My husband heard it all and came to help between songs," Alice recalls wistfully. "That was the worst Sunday of my life. I was in the car sobbing when one of the Co-op women came over and said, 'I understand how overwhelming this is. You need support.' She was right. I had thought I'd be a super mom, but I knew I couldn't handle this all by myself."

Malls weren't Sid Morrow's favorite place to take her children. "I hated, *hated,* taking my kids to the mall. I didn't like what the mall did to them. Some kids have a really high mall tolerance; my kids would be all over." But the decision to join the Co-op came after realizing how Sid's no-escape life was affecting the entire family. "My kids would follow me into the bathroom, pull my hair. They were just like monkeys around my neck all day. Then my husband would come home and I was in no mood to be touched. After I joined the Co-op, I had time alone and a change of surroundings. He could never understand why I was in such a good mood after getting away for a moment to myself."

Moms have plenty of untapped goodwill to spread around. It is just a matter of giving moms more options so they can manage their priorities.

Sid Morrow, mother of three, struggled with being pulled in different directions. "We made a decision to take a big cut in living expenses so I could be at home with our children. I made the choice to be home, and then I spent all day working around them trying to get things done. It didn't make sense. I used to volunteer and contribute. I had to drop out of things that were important to me. After joining a Co-op, I can do those extras without putting a strain on the family."

Sandra Bedford realized that she had been a mom for a really long time. "Everything I did was kid related. I was going crazy. I would pay a sitter to take care of my kids so I could go to school to help other kids bake cookies. That seemed really dumb. My friend was always talking about activities she did. She made it sound like she had a normal life that didn't have anything to do with kids. I asked her how she found the time. Her answer was the Baby-sitting Co-op."

15

Smart Mom's At a Glance

The Best Reasons for a Baby-sitting Co-op

- If you think you have adequate baby-sitter coverage—you are probably in serious denial. When was the last time you found a sitter, on a moment's notice, to watch your kids so you could read a book at a coffee shop?

- Friends and family can only do so much—they need a break too.

- If two or three sitters are good, 10 or 12 should be that much better.

- What is the best gift you can give a mother of preschoolers? Some moms are new to the area. Some are desperately isolated. The reason to do a Baby-sitting Co-op is one-part about you, but one hundred-parts about other moms. Over the years, dozens of moms will benefit because of your effort to start a Co-op. If you have been invited to participate in a friend's Co-op—do it. If not, study the merit of bringing moms together in your own Baby-sitting Co-op.

Out of all moms who will benefit from a simple Baby-sitting Co-op over the years, you happen to be in the right place, at the right time, with the right book in your hand to make it happen for everyone. What a coincidence. You must be special—you must be the one to get things moving. It is a piece of cake. You can do it. Go for it.

Chapter 3

A Safe and Caring Environment: Tips for Protective Moms

"I am a protective mom. I would never leave my kids with a stranger."
—Tory Karmic, mother of three

How can a Baby-sitting Co-op pass the test for the protective mom? The answer is the one-year-trial. Everyone wants a safe and caring environment for the kids. Co-op moms understand if you want to join their existing Co-op just to check things out and meet other moms. If you are thinking about participating in an existing Co-op—do it. No need to become active until the time is right for you—one week, one month, or one year.

It is a good idea to join (or start) the Co-op well in advance of when you might really need it—like right before your fifth child is born. By most accounts, moms gradually make lasting friendships. And then you will have more loving baby-sitters than you ever thought possible.

Some moms are happy with having their kids with them at all times. It is not easy to manage, but many moms do a wonderful job making it all work. Separation anxiety is a real thing for children—and moms too. Even so, most moms find merit in the idea that both mom and child can benefit by learning to let go just a little. In the long run, too much protection is no protection at all. Sometimes less is more. In any case, move ahead at your own pace.

For the protective mom with a touch of separation anxiety, you will know when the time is right to call for a sitter. Remember one thing— if you give yourself a break, you will be refreshed and energized to care for your family. The Co-op is a good place to start gradually.

Once you decide to do the one-year-trial, you will find lots of ways to ease into the Co-op—be sure to go to all the meetings. As a new participant you are the featured guest. Other moms want to get to know you, too.

There are a few things that you can do to speed things up. One idea is to sit for other moms first. That way you get to know both the moms and the kids, too.

Another idea is to invite a mom and her kids over for coffee and dessert. Perhaps she will return the favor and invite you to her home so you can see for yourself where the children will play.

If you are using a sitter for the first time, it's okay to make it a short outing. You can turn down a sitter for any reason. You will always be working through the Co-op Secretary so it is not a personal thing.

Another idea is to ask some of your friends to join the Co-op. (Or think about doing a new Co-op of your own.) How you work it out is up to you.

Smart Mom's At a Glance

For the Protective Mom

● Do the one-year-trial to see how things work and to get to know the other moms. You are just an observer until you want to become active.

● Start gradually—request a sitter that you know and make it a short sit for only a couple of hours.

● Ask your friends to participate—find quality people you can rely on.

● Take every opportunity to get to know the Co-op moms. The meetings are fun time to get together—be sure to attend.

● Offer to sit for other moms first—you can meet the moms and children on your own turf and earn points at the same time.

● Look at the bigger picture. A Co-op will give you more options so you can better focus on what is important to you and your family. Children need playmates and you need time out without the added stress of tracking down a baby-sitter.

Safety First...

"When I was asked to join, the Co-op sent three moms to my home for a safety visit. We discussed baby-proofing my home and we went over other possible hazards. I was impressed with the safety check."
—Cyndy Metz, mother of two

Of course you are concerned about safety and a caring place for your child! Co-op moms have discovered some fun ways to deal with these things.

The Smart Mom's Baby-sitting rules call for a home safety visit for each new mom. This is necessary to get to know new moms and to keep everyone thinking about safety. The home visit is short and simple. Three Co-op moms will make an appointment to see your home and ask to be shown the area of the home where the children will play. They will want to talk about possible safety hazards like weapons, an unfenced yard, a busy street, a swimming pool, animals, or medicines. They also go over how the Co-op works and answer questions.

All moms are aware that stuff happens. The best thing moms can do for each other is to prevent problems before they happen. Everyone is responsible to be sure that your Co-op discusses safety at every meeting. Launch a spring cleaning and baby-proofing program. Invite someone to a meeting to teach self-defense or CPR. Make sure your own house is baby proofed! Be creative. Think safety.

The moms of the University Place Baby-sitting Co-op came up with some interesting safety tips. Moms have lots of personal experiences to share. Your Co-op moms will have lots of safety ideas to record. Be sure your Co-op lists the safety tips in the Leaders Workbook so others will benefit in the future.

The Authorization for Medical Treatment Form

This form provides the sitter with emergency phone numbers, and the name of the family doctor. The form also identifies other special medical conditions like allergies that sitters should know. Moms are required to have a current medical release form for every participant in the Co-op. The sitter must get the release form out of her file before the sit for handy reference in case of an emergency.

Finding Reliable Participants

Everyone must understand what the Co-op is, and what it is not. On the one hand, Baby-sitting Co-ops usually have a process to do home safety checks and to learn more about new participants before a new

Smart Mom's TIPS

Safety Insight from the University Place Co-op

- Toddlers will often lean against a window screen even if they are on the third floor. Be sure to remove window screens or secure the window.

- There are all kinds of portable desk lamps and utility lights. Some have high temperature lamps. A lamp on placed on the floor can act as a captivating projector of color and patterns from the fabric of a child's dress. Be sure to secure the lamps to avoid igniting clothing.

- Some toddlers are escape artists of enormous strength. Toddlers have been known to kick out a picket from the side of their crib. The crib may still look okay but a child may get their head caught after its body has slipped through. Repair the crib promptly.

- Little booties have handy elastic collars that help keep the boot on the foot. The elastic can apply tourniquet-like pressure if it slips down stretching over the heel. It's hard to catch because the boots often have decorative pleats.

- With the large number of products in the medicine cabinet that look alike, it is not surprising to hear stories of moms mistakenly using mosquito insect spray instead of an antibiotic spray, or ear drops instead of eye drops. It pays to double check and keep medicine cabinets organized.

mom is invited to join. On the other hand, each mom must never rely on the Co-op for screening of other participants. Each participant must understand that the Co-op only *facilitates* baby-sitting exchanges. The Co-op does not *certify* the character of its participants, the quality of their home environments or guarantee a problem-free sit.

Seniority does not exist in the Co-op. Your concerns have equal weight. If you are concerned about someone or a situation, it is up to you to follow up with the Leader. Verify the problem and work to resolve it.

Each September the Leader will ask you to renew your registration. This is a good time to encourage each other to take a moment to think about safety and the legal stuff—like verifying that everyone's homeowner's insurance is current. Take advantage of the special September meeting and find ways to have meaningful and productive discussions about safety, liability, and Co-op standards.

Chapter 4

From the Heart: Roundtable Stories from Co-op Moms

Gini Walker knew it was time to call for help when she lost her two preschoolers in the clothes rack. "I didn't know where they were. They wouldn't make a sound and thought it was real funny. Then a saleslady scolded me for letting the kids play in the clothes rack. I don't mind taking my kids places, but I *really* enjoy having the option of going by myself if I want to."

"I can do it myself," was the mode Patty Johnson was in the day she took her child to the mall. She was pregnant with her second and didn't expect the tantrum. However, the child decided she wouldn't sit in the

The University Place Baby-sitting Co-op serves its participants in a variety of ways. They get to keep doctor appointments without distraction, shop without children reaching for things or throwing tantrums, set up lunch appointments with friends or just take time out for themselves.

stroller and then escalated her rage into a tantrum. Patty tells it this way. "I picked her up over my shoulder so she wouldn't kick my pregnant stomach. Legs were flying as I waddled my pregnant body from one end of the mall to the other and out to the car. It was not a good day." She soon joined the Co-op and was surprised when she took the younger child to the mall the first time when she was about four. "Oh

Mom, look at all this stuff," the child said. It was then that Patty realized how the Co-op had allowed her freedom to shop without children.

Not only was Patty able to shop at the mall on weekdays, but she realized "how beneficial it was for my kids to go to other homes. Now they go just for playtime, not a sit."

Sandra Bedford had problems with malls and her four children. "When I put the kids in the cart, one would just scream," she recalls. "I would say nope, not today. . . and leave. I figured that the store had video cameras and they must have a bunch of shots of me coming in the door, yanking my kids out of the cart and taking off again. They must have wondered who that crazy mom was.

Jenna Floyd found the most helpful time was when she had eye surgery. "Another helpful time was when it was so cold out I didn't want to be hauling the kids around with me. I called the Co-op! That group ended up being a friendship kind of group that I hadn't even expected."

Tory Karmic says she likes the freedom the Co-op affords her. "With the Co-op, I have become more peaceful, knowing I have a set time I can count on. I don't have to go with the flow; I can count on a block of time. And that helps me a lot."

Molly Evans called the Co-op a lifesaver. "That was over 10 years ago. Another mom with boys the same age kept mine busy; I loved it. The Co-op participants enjoyed all kinds of parties. We made quilts for each new baby until that got to be too much. I looked forward to the

Christmas and Easter parties—a nice way to meet other moms. I've been out of the Co-op awhile now, but I still see a few of them. We became very close."

Not only is time scarce for many parents with young children, but so is money. Child-care facilities can be very expensive, especially drop-in daycare. "With teen sitters unavailable during the day, the Co-op just seems to be a realistic answer to the problem of daytime tempo-rary child sitting," says Jean Cunningham mother of three. "There's no money exchanged. It's all done with points."

"The meetings were more like a night out with friends," says Linda Hayley. I remember when one participant was diagnosed with a ter-rible disease, the Co-op brought hot meals to her. It went beyond baby-sitting; that's the memory that lasts for me. We each gave her points so she didn't have to worry about a sitter for her children."

Co-op moms have many stories to tell. All will agree that the Co-op has been a *small* effort that makes life easier in a *big* way. If you are just starting out new, the Co-op moms of University Place encourage you to immediately call for lots of sits so you get into enough debt to be called by the Secretary to sit for others. If you are not getting a call from the Secretary—you are not using the Co-op enough.

2

How Do I Start
a Baby-sitting Co-op
from Scratch?

Chapter 5

Time Is Limited: Up and Running after One Meeting with Three Moms

"It's so easy to start, you ask people you know who live in your area. Invite them over. It just makes so much sense. You get the break you need and deserve while your child is being cared for by another loving mom. Who wouldn't want to be involved?"
—Jean Cunningham, mother of three

Thank you for being the one to start a Smart Mom's Baby-sitting Co-op! Starting a Baby-sitting Co-op is not rocket science. If you've traded baby-sitting with a few friends, you have already started! The Smart Mom's Baby-sitting Co-op system just adds a touch of organization to what you are already doing. The idea is to add a few more moms to your circle of friends to make sure everyone will have a sitter every time they want.

Doing a Co-op is not about joining a mega-organization or electing officers. It is more like getting together to play volleyball. There a few rules, a few responsibilities, and lots of fun.

What you have here is more than the pages you see in front of you. You have the beginnings of something big. With these materials you have everything you need to help bring relief to moms who seldom get a break and seem to be on duty 24-hours a day. You will soon make a very meaningful difference in the day-to-day lives of moms just like you.

So, have fun tearing into this book. Think about what your work here today might look like 20 years from now. Consider for a moment the idea that your daughter and grandchild may join the Baby-sitting Co-op you are starting today. Take pride in being the first person to begin a wonderful service for the moms in your community. Have a nice cup of tea and a peaceful moment to celebrate this beginning. You are now making a little bit of history.

If you have held this book in your hands for more than a few minutes, you have already passed the test. You can do it. You have the inter-est, you are aware of the need, and you understand the benefits a Baby-sitting Co-op can produce. You will not be on your own. If you follow the steps, it will be you and three other moms who get things moving. And don't worry about the cost. Everyone will buy their own Co-op Handbook and share other expenses.

Smart Mom's TIPS

Let the Handbook Do the Work For You

No need to be a salesperson. The best way to invite a mom to participate is to let the Smart Mom's Baby-sitting Co-op Handbook do the explaining for you. Everything is in the Handbook. You will need three other moms to help with the startup. Take the plunge—get a Handbook for yourself and three extras. When you invite a mom to participate lend them a Handbook on the spot. Reimburse yourself for the cost of the Handbooks when you collect participation fees. Getting books up-front will save time and add momentum to your efforts.

The Secret to Success

The secret to success is discovering one simple thing—you often get exactly what you ask for. If you share the Baby-sitting Co-op idea with other moms and ask them to *think about it*, that is exactly what they will do. They will *think about it*. If you tell them you have decided to do a Baby-sitting Co-op and ask them to come to your home for dessert to *do* it with you, they will come prepared to *do* a Baby-sitting Co-op.

The subtle difference between asking someone to *think about it*, instead of asking friends over to *do it*, can mean the difference between talking about a good idea or doing a good idea.

When you invite someone to *do* a Baby-sitting Co-op with you, they will not make the mistake of thinking you just want their advice about the idea. When you tell a friend you have *decided* you will do a Baby-sitting Co-op, then everything is clear. They will understand you are ready to move ahead. They will know their job is to look over the Smart Mom's Baby-sitting Co-op Handbook to see if a Co-op will work for them.

This approach takes the pressure off your friends. It is only fair. They will know the whole thing does not depend on them. It's okay if they want to pass. It is great if they want to be part of the startup.

31

"But I Don't Have the Time"

> *"The jobs rotate among participants. It's a long time between turns. Being the Leader or Secretary takes very little time. I do Co-op sits when I'm planning to be home anyway. I often get more done around the house because my child has a playmate."*
>
> *—Judy Manza, mother of five*

We know that your time is filled with an endless routine of diapers, cleaning, cooking and shopping. There are only a few moments in the day to do something for yourself. We are honored you are taking this time to look things over. Here is what you can expect over the first six months:

Browse through the Co-op Handbook and Workbooks:	1 hour
Invite three friends over for start-up and planning:	2 hours
Three regular meetings, over six months:	4 hours
Home safety visit for each new participant:	4 hours
	12 hours

Your One-and-Only Startup Meeting

Before we begin with the specifics of how to startup your Co-op, it is important give you some straight talk about what needs to happen to get things up and running.

To start a Baby-sitting Co-op you need yourself and three others to do the 'one and only startup meeting'. The purpose of the meeting is to learn how to register participants, to practice how the Secretary keeps track of points, and to get set to invite other moms to participate. These will be accomplished by following the steps in this chapter.

After you finish the steps, you will be instructed to do a role-play scenario to practice how a sit is requested and recorded. With all four participants working things out, it will not take long to understand the daily operation of the Co-op or the roles of the Leader and the Secretary.

The forms and rules that make a Co-op work are really quite simple. Do not be surprised if you buzz through the steps in twenty minutes or less. Then what?

It is important to have a good discussion. Ask questions and find answers. The Handbook will answer most procedural questions. You can rely on the checklist at the end of this chapter to provide other important topics of discussion. It is your Co-op. Not all questions can be answered in a book. Be ready to work together to create some answers to some of your own questions and interests.

Although a Co-op starts with only four, the idea is to spend the first part of the meeting learning about how things work and the other part of the meeting planning on inviting others to participate. It is important to review Chapters 15 and 16 to understand the steps of how to bring on a new participant.

Enough talk, it's time to get started.

Eight Steps to Start-up

1 Find three moms in addition to yourself and supply them each with a Baby-sitting Co-op Handbook. (In time, all participants will need a Co-op Handbook and each Co-op group will need a Leader Workbook and a Secretary Workbook.) Be sure to obtain the Handbooks and the Workbooks so they are available at your startup meeting. The workbooks can be downloaded free from the Smart

Mom's web site. Call 1-888-974-2667 for the current e-mail address and information to order Co-op handbooks. Be sure to put the workbook materials into two three-ring binders.

2 Find your Co-op identification number on the cover of the Leader Workbook and write it on the front cover of your Co-op Handbook.

3 Fill out the Leader and Secretary rotation lists in the Leader Workbook so everyone will know who will be the next Secretary and the next Leader.

4 Register yourselves into your own co-op. A Registration Form is located in the back of each Co-op Handbook. Be sure to write the Co-op ID number on your Registration Form. Read the form and Chapters 16 and 17 to see why registration is an important aspect of doing a Co-op. Keep the original registration forms in the Leader Workbook.

- It is the Leaders job to see that each mom has a copy of the Authorization of Medical Treatment form from all other moms.
- It is the Leader's job to send a copy of the registrations to Smart Mom's Co., c/o Tukwila Book Publishers, 8408 S. 18th Street, W., Tacoma, WA 98465.

5 Record your names in the Participant Directory in the Leader's Workbook. Make a note to call your insurance agent to request proof of homeowner's insurance with a minimum liability of $100,000. (Insurance is a reasonable precaution.)

6 The Co-op needs funds to buy stamps and get-well cards. The suggested amount for the participation fee is six to eight dollars a year. You may decide to increase this the first year to cover the cost of buying the Baby-sitting Co-op Handbooks. It is the Leader's job to collect participation fees. Keep the money in a pencil pouch in the Leader Workbook.

7 The Treasury Worksheet in the Leader's Workbook is for recording deposit totals—not each payment received. Be sure to record a date in the box next to their name in the Participant Directory to indicate payment recieved.

8 Start a new "Participant Balance Sheet" in the Secretary's Workbook for each participant. This will be used to keep track of points.

Record your names on the Co-op Start-up Certificate provided in the Leader Workbook. (You are the founding mothers of your Co-op!) Also follow the instructions to record the street boundaries of the Co-op.

Now turn to Appendix A to follow the flow chart steps to learn how things work.

Once you know how things work, it is important to add a few new participants in the first six months. If you don't use the Co-op, you may lose it!

At the end of this meeting each mom should understand:
- How to do the home visit and enroll a new mom (Chapter 16).
- How the Secretary records points (Chapter 13).
- How to call for a sitter (Chapter 3).
- How to use the Handbook as a reference.

At the end of this meeting everyone will have:
- Defined the Co-op boundaries.
- Completed registration.
- Practiced the role-play flow chart Appendix A.
- Decided on the First Leader and Secretary.
- Set goals for inviting other moms.
- Confirmed the next meeting time and place.

Congratulations! You are now a proud participant of your own Baby-sitting Co-op! Do something special to celebrate this beginning—you did it!

Smart Mom's TIPS

Discussion Checklist

✔ Have we completed all the start-up steps?

✔ Does the Leader have a copy of our registrations to send in?

✔ Do we know who will be the next Leader and Secretary?

✔ The Leader's term runs from January to June and July to December—will this shorten the term of the first Leader?

✔ We need to practice the Co-op system. Are we ready to use the Co-op with just the original four when we want a sitter?

✔ We really need to find other moms to join. Is the leader ready to follow the steps once we find an interested mom? Are we ready to do the home visit process together? Who will watch our kids at that time?

✔ What are our standards for inviting a mom to participate?

✔ The Handbook suggests certain meeting dates. Are we ready to go with these dates? When is the next regular meeting? Where?

✔ How can we make the next meeting a success for the new moms?

✔ We can do most of our work over the phone. Can we save other business for when we meet for home visits for new moms?

✔ We should not panic if we go weeks without any Co-op activity but how long will it take to get up and running? What are our goals for adding new moms? How do we keep from dropping the ball?

✔ Are we missing something? The Co-op seems to be just a couple of notebooks for the Leader and Secretary. Besides a few meetings is that all there is?

Chapter 6

Special Startup Tips for Large Groups: Option A or Option B

"The great thing about this Baby-sitting Co-op is that it can work independently as a small home-based program or it can be integrated with existing group functions. Either way, the Co-op works on auto-pilot."
—Sid Morrow, mother of three

If you belong to a church group or organization with lots of other moms, you may be thinking about how the whole group can start a Baby-sitting Co-op together. The answer is that there is nothing to it. There are lots of benefits that a Co-op might add to your existing group.

A Baby-sitting Co-op is a new and different framework for working together. It is a catalyst that energizes moms to get things happening. Synergy is a wonderful thing. A baby-sitting Co-op can add a rich dimension to what moms are already doing in an existing group or organization. Co-op moms are in the problem-solving mode—you will find they are in contact with each other more often and they trade sits more frequently than before the Co-op.

A Baby-sitting Co-op Has Staying Power
Programs and services come and go. Few can claim they have survived 20 years. Fewer still can claim they have thrived without an institu-

tional anchor or the pioneering individual to pull the load. The Smart Mom's Baby-sitting Co-op system is based on an independent neighborhood Co-op which has been passed from mom to mom for many years. Over the years, the University Place Co-op is sustained by the desire of moms to help each other in the most sensible way possible.

How many Co-ops do I need for my group? Home-based or site-based?

The most important thing to consider when looking at how many Co-ops to launch is the fact that moms will trade sitting with moms they know well and who live close to home. The way you split things up is up to you. You can have one Co-op or many—the cost is the same. If you start with small groups, groups can be combined in the future.

Co-op moms need to be able to get together to meet new moms and to develop new friendships. If this already happens within your existing group then there is less need for having home-based meetings. On the other hand, many large groups can be impersonal because of their size. Large groups may welcome the idea of smaller home-based Co-ops as a way to break the ice and make things more comfortable for new moms.

As a Program Director for a large group of moms, your job is simply to introduce the Smart Mom's Baby-sitting Co-op. It will be the moms who will make it happen—they just need to read the Handbook and follow the steps. There are two ways to introduce a Baby-sitting Co-op to a large group.

Option A: Low Profile, Sowing the Seeds
The Co-op Handbook is the best thing to use to answer questions and advertise the concept. Get a few of the Co-op handbooks and hand

them out to a few moms with some encouraging words. The idea is for each mom to form a Co-op group. Any mom can do it. If each mom follows the steps, she will look for three friends in her area and get started. Everything will be finalized at their first meeting. From there, she and her three friends will begin to invite others near where they live to join them. Option A takes no effort. With a little follow-up you will be certain to produce results. Just keep passing the Co-op Handbooks on to the next mom until you find a mom who wants to do it and is willing to find three people to help. Home-based Co-ops function best with 10 to 20 participants.

Option B: Proactive Approach

Make a short announcement to the entire group. Tell them you are taking orders for the Smart Mom's Baby-sitting Co-op Handbook for anyone who is interested for review purposes only—no obligation. This will provide you with your first indication of how many will participate.

After each mom has had a chance to review the Smart Mom's Baby-sitting Co-op Handbook, the group can make an informed decision to proceed or not.

Anyone not wanting to participate can return her Handbook to you and you can send it back for a refund. (You will find that most moms who ask you to order a Co-op Handbook on a review basis will be interested enough to move ahead after they have a chance to look it over.) Those that didn't order the first time will scramble for the few leftover books. If you still have leftover books they can normally be returned to the place of purchase for a refund. Be sure to confirm the refund policy of the bookstore or contact the publisher.

Once you know who wants to participate in a Baby-sitting Co-op, the next thing is to decide if you want to have lots of small Co-ops or have a single larger Co-op. The choice is yours.

Home-based Baby-sitting Co-ops

If you go with the small-group home-based approach, count how many moms are interested and learn where they live. Group moms into groups of about ten according to what would be sensible street boundaries for each Co-op. An overlap of the boundaries is not a problem. (The boundaries are there to make sure moms do not have to drive too far for a sitter.) It might be a good idea to get a map and mark down each home so you can see how to create the boundaries.

The Task-force Option

Get a commitment from a few moms to spend a half-hour reviewing the Co-op Handbook plus a half-hour to discuss the idea together. Their assignment is to make a recommendation to the group about whether the group should do a Baby-sitting Co-op or not. A good task-force will return a verdict of either yes or no. If this happens ask them to return to deliberate until they reach a verdict—or do option A or B above.

Great things can be built on good friendships strengthened by the real help and support that makes a meaningful difference. Go with what works. The sky is the limit.

There are many different ways to run a baby-sitting Co-op. Your Co-op can change the guidelines to fit your needs and values. The University Place Co-op tried many things over the years. Perhaps Co-op business can be tacked on to the end of other meetings or activities. A meeting of five or 10 minutes is all that is needed for participants to coordinate their calendars. This will reduce the number of calls the Secretary must handle to coordinate sits.

If you are considering doing a Baby-sitting Co-op for your group of mothers of preschoolers it is important to read Secton 1. This chapter highlights how a Co-op can make a meaningful difference in the day to day lives of mothers of preschoolers.

Smart Mom's TIPS

Start With a Splash

- The executive's way to speed things up—take the liberty to order Co-op Handbooks for half of your group of mothers of preschoolers.

- Give them time to review the Handbook.

- If they do not want to participate—they turn in the book. If they want to keep their options open or move ahead—they buy the book from you.

- Return excess books to the publisher or bookstore for a refund or order more depending on demand.

- Determine how many Co-ops you want and identify some street boundaries to keep driving time short. This is best done by marking each home on a map before deciding how many Co-ops are needed and what areas they will serve.

- Identify one person for each Co-op area and have her follow the Eight Steps to Start up in Chapter 5.

- At the next opportunity, ask your group to make sure everyone who wants to participate has found a Co-op near their home.

Benefits of a Large Group Starting a Co-op

- Moms do not have the support structure and time out a Baby-sitting Co-op will produce. The Co-op is a catalyst for moms to shift into the problem-solving mode—not only for baby-sitting but for lots of other things too.

- A Baby-sitting Co-op will allow moms to volunteer their time or attend the important functions sponsored by school or church. Moms will be free to schedule time out.

- A Baby-sitting Co-op is a tried and true way to reach out to moms. A Baby-sitting Co-op can be the centerpiece of a logical progression of new program offerings to serve an ever-increasing participant base. If you have a visionary plan to attract new people—a Co-op is a must.

- Baby-sitting Co-ops can be scaled up (or down) to meet the needs of your large group. A Co-op can be highly integrated into your existing organization, or the Co-op can be completely independent. The choice is yours. Either way, you are the sponsor, your job is limited to planting the seed. Nothing more.

- A Smart Mom's Baby-sitting Co-op is self-starting, self-governing, and self-sustaining. The moms do it all by themselves. A Baby-sitting Co-op will stay in the background and will enhance your programs, not compete with them. You and the participants have complete ownership and may customize the Co-op to reflect your needs and values.

- The cost of a Co-op is minimal. Participants must buy their own Co-op Handbook. Participants are not roped into a bunch of commitments. You can have one Co-op or many—the cost is the same.

3

How Do I Get the Most from My Co-op?

Chapter 7

Date and Dine-out More Often: The Secret About Evening Sits

Planning a night out together is a good way to honor yourself for an endless job well done. Much of life's happiness is one's own responsibility. Many of us really do need to care for ourselves as we would hope to have others care for us. Begin by being your own best friend. This means it is wise to take time to enjoy the small pleasures. Find comfort in the simple things—a cup of tea, or some good music. It also means to plan your own date once in a while.

It would be wonderful if your husband was able to surprise you by arranging special dates all the time. But do a reality check—if he cannot remember to take the garbage out or pick up after himself, chances are he will not know when things in your complicated life are all lined up to give you the energy, the interest, and the baby-sitter coverage needed for a special date. If you are counting on him to sort it all out, you may be in for a long wait. Do not take the risk. Take action.

For some women, planning one's own date is like buying one's own birthday present—something does not feel right but there are some advantages. Just explain to him that the flowers are from him—it was a nice touch. The lovely card he sent was very romantic (let him read what you wrote to yourself.) Be sure to thank him for making a reservation at your favorite restaurant—how thoughtful of him!

When you arrive at your destination, remain in the car. He, from across the parking lot, puzzled and bewildered, will then turn to look at you still seated in the car. He will then realize it's his job to open the car door for you. (You might need to point at the door.) His sudden insight, not to forget the effort to open the door, is enough for him to take ownership of the entire date. He will take full credit from this single act of participation.

Years from now he will proudly remind you, "Remember that time I got you flowers, and took you to your special restaurant? Remember the card I got you?"

The secret to dating is to do it on a regular schedule. Eventually, your husband will think it was his idea and think of ways to make nights out special for you.

Dating regularly is easy to arrange when other Co-op moms are also interested in a night out. Sid Morrow, mother of three, tells how evening sits worked for her. "Before the Co-op, my husband and I would trade time out. Then we would argue about who gave whom time off; it was tit-for-tat. With the Co-op, I was making more time *for* my husband, rather than needing his time so I could get things done. He was glad when I didn't have to run out to do chores after he got home. And when he wanted us to go out together, we'd just call a Co-op sitter."

Sid touches on one of the most important parts of doing evening sits, "In our Co-op, evening sits racked up additional points. My husband stayed home with our children while I watched kids at another mom's home. What a relief to be at someone else's home and have quiet time to myself with all the kids safely tucked in bed. There's something about being in a different surrounding where I could take a breath and unwind."

Sid points out. "Half the time I'd use the Co-op points to give my husband a break." Then Sid hesitates with a big smile as she confesses, "Okay, okay, maybe he didn't get exactly half—but I was doing all the work. The points I earned during the day were for myself. I'd use the points I earned in the evening for dates with my husband. When I was away at an evening sit, he would do his part and take over bedtime chores at home so he deserved something. The best part was to see my husband get closer to our kids. If I was there, the kids would go for Mom. If I was away, Dad got a chance to get to know the kids in his own way."

Doing the Evening Sit—Great Therapy for Mom

The secret to more dating and dining out is to get Co-op moms interested in evening sits. Evening sits only work when moms understand the advantages and are willing to take the sit. Evening sits can be rewarding as a sitter too. Make it a time to treat yourself. Buy yourself a magazine or bring a good book to read when the kids are in bed.

We all get comfortable in our routine at home. Moms like to protect their evening because it is the only relief time they have. Even so, new surroundings can be great therapy. It is important for moms to overcome the exhaustion of a long day and make the effort. Try a few evening sits—and of course dating too. Evening sits can be a good thing for the Co-op—and a great thing for a relationship.

Smart Mom's At a Glance

Evening Sits

- If an evening sit is requested the sitter should do the sit at the children's home.

- Children are more likely to get a good night's sleep in their own bed.

- Couples are more likely to go out on dates if it is easy on the kids.

- Dates are more fun—no worry about getting back early to take a teenage sitter home.

- Evening sitters soon discover they like the quiet time and new surroundings.

- New dads report that when mom does evening sits out, time alone with the kids is a good experience even if it is more work.

- Did someone mention going out on more dates?

Chapter 8

Get Into Time-out: Dial the Secretary

The Co-op can be used for anything you want—even to treat yourself to some time out during the day. You will have plenty of errands to run. You will have dozens of appointments to keep. The Co-op is not only for getting more things done. It is mostly about taking a break.

Do not worry about any paperwork when you request a sitter. Just call the Secretary and she will find a sitter and take care of everything.

You start with zero points. When you use a sitter you spend points. It is perfectly normal to have negative points. That's the way it is designed. It is best for new participants to just dive in and request a sit right away. If you do not know all the participants, make a special request for a sitter that you already know.

Some moms just like to get out and meet other people.

Errands, appointments, or any other form of business are not allowed the first time you use the Co-op—no exceptions.

Go ahead. Think of something special to do for yourself and then call the Secretary to arrange the sitter. Take a moment to recharge. You are not a machine. When you take care of yourself, you are also taking care of your family.

Judy Manza is one of those. "I call this a great way to meet other moms and introduce your children to a host of new playmates," says the mother of five." The Co-op has enabled me to volunteer at my children's elementary school or shop without having to pay for a baby sitter."

Linda Hayley, mother of two, recalls how she had problems planning appointments before she found the Co-op. "How nice to be able to set up a lunch date without having to check first. My kids don't have handy grandparents, so the Co-op was definitely the answer for me."

Time out is also important for emergency situations. Tory Karmic valued the Co-op most after her third child was born. She had gone through a pregnancy where she was sick all the time and "backed out of life" for six months. Then the new baby needed extra care. She decided to reserve a time each week just for herself. "I like a sched-ule. I shop, take a nap, anything, and it's really awesome." During the time right after the birth of that third child, Tory knew she was going into "point debt," but she figured it was worth it. As soon as things quieted down, she made up the debt.

Be sure to bring extra clothes and have the children ready for the sitter. Bag lunches and snacks should be arranged before the sit. You know the drill. Never drop off a kid with a dirty diaper. Take care to plan ahead.

Life is short. If you agree with the idea that the Co-op is made to help bring peace-of-mind and sanity to mothers of preschoolers, then it is important that you make the decision to re-engineer *all* areas of stress. It is much less stressful to be early and enjoy a moment to visit than to drop off the kids in a rush of chaos. No more rushing. Do your best to be early.

Smart Mom's RULES

When You Request a Sitter

1. The requester should call the Secretary 48 hours or more in advance. The Secretary will record the sit request in her workbook and will call around to find a sitter. The Secretary will call the participant with the most negative points first.

2. For those sits needed on short notice, the requester finds the sitter herself and reports the sit to the Secretary as soon as possible.

3. If you are 80 points in debt—it's time to start digging out of the hole.

4. You must call to confirm the sit with the sitter the night before the sit.

5. If you cancel a sit, you must call to notify both the sitter and the Secretary.

Finally, each mom must remember she has the option to refuse a sitter for any reason. Plan to take your time getting to know the other moms before you have them sit for your kids. The requester must reject sitters that are strangers. By this rule only trusted friends are allowed to sit for friends.

Chapter 9

Be a Sitter: Just Say When

The Secretary will call you to see if you are available to do a sit. The Secretary always calls Co-op moms who have the most negative points first. If you are a new participant, you begin with zero points so you will not normally be the first called to sit. If you would like to do a few sits, just call the Secretary and let her know. She may be able to direct some your way.

When the Secretary makes the arrangement, there is no feeling of obligation by either party. The Co-op is business-like. If you get called to sit and you have other plans, it is okay to say no. Someone else will usually be available.

"I used to feel I would be imposing too much on a friend if I asked them to watch my kids," said Lori Paul, mother of two. "But that's what the Co-op is for! We're together for the prime purpose of caring for each other's children. I do not hesitate to call for a sit."

Sandra Bedford likes sitting for other kids. "I get more done with extra kids. I stenciled my kitchen with six kids in the house. My neighbor thought I was nuts."

Moms report they like having playmates over for their children. Many children form strong friendships as part of their Co-op experiences.

These are important. A child who is very timid about her first swimming lesson will be more willing if she discovers a Co-op friend in a swim suit ready to jump in. The Co-op is about time-out for mom—but another advantage is about quality experiences for the kids.

Sid Morrow points out, "I plan something for the kids when I sit with them—watercolor painting or other hand work they can take home. I wanted to show evidence of good-mom stuff. Co-op time is for the kids; I try harder to plan ahead for the snack instead of waiting for the children to get grumpy. I try to make it good for the kids because I want moms to feel good about having me watch their children."

Tory Karmic has three children. "When I asked friends to sit, I felt like it wasn't an equal trade because I had more kids. I felt I was taking advantage of my friends." The Co-op has bonus points for extra kids. Now Tory understands that moms want to sit for her kids to earn more points.

The proof is in the results. Sandra Bedford sums it up this way. "I know that without a doubt, in a pinch, I could call anyone to get help for anything. I'm not scared to ask, and neither is anybody else. I want to help and I want to serve. You need to be bold enough to ask. You can't expect others to know when help is needed. I will help anybody if they ask. If you cannot help people, if you cannot serve others, why are you breathing? That's a benefit of the Co-op. I know that in a bind we can work things out with each other's help."

Smart Mom's RULES

When You Are a Sitter

1. A participant with 80 points credit may not sit unless no other participant is available. It is time to enjoy the fruit of your labor. Spend some points.

2. The sitter must never leave children unattended. She must never leave the children under the care of a non-participant. Spouses and relatives are not participants of the Co-op.

3. The sitter must notify the requester ahead of time if she will transport children or leave the house.

4. The sitter must call the Secretary and report her actual hours and number of children to be cared for. The Secretary will figure the points on the point chart. See Chapter 13. Make sure you report your hours within a week or you will lose two points to the Secretary.

5. A participant may sit for two Co-op families provided permission from the original requester is obtained.

6. The sitter is not required to feed, bathe, or dress children unless arranged prior to the sit.

7. Should the sitter cancel, she should call other participants to find another sitter for the requester if possible. She loses a two points to the requester if she cancels less than three days before the sit.

8. If the sitter forgets a sit or otherwise defaults, the estimated points for the sit are transferred to the requester.

Chapter 10

Success Together: Ground Rules That Work

Too many rules can be just as troublesome as not enough rules. The Smart Mom's Baby-sitting Co-op achieves a good balance.

Karen Bream considers the best thing about the University Place Co-op to be "the like-minded, like-valued women whom I can trust. They seem like lifelong relationships. Our Co-op takes very little effort. The rules help eliminate lots of confusion and extra work." Karen is the mother of three.

Erica Bissett, mother of two, recalls how well her Co-op ran. "The rules are part of its success. It's detailed. Some may want it more laid back—I think it would fizzle. It was friendly, but there was a business side. It allows us to address more issues that we might avoid if it were just social."

The rules from a book can only do so much. A successful Co-op is also built on simple understandings between participants. Be sure to have a good discussion, vote, then write down the new rules in the Leader Workbook. Rules help prevent conflict. If the there is a dispute, it is probably a good sign that the Co-op could benefit from clarifying the underlying issue.

Your Co-op must also take time to think of rules and methods to make sure new participants are team players and are reliable. Co-op moms should also spend some time making rules about safety issues. It is a good idea to create your own safety checklist for the home visits and baby-proofing. The Handbook calls for one home visit for new moms. Your Co-op may want to do a safety visit each year.

A Co-op may survive for generations. It would be unfortunate if a simple unresolved conflict resulted in the end of a Co-op that has benefited so many over the years. It pays to have rules that can help a Co-op sort through a problem. For many Co-ops, once participants understand how the Co-op works, the tough rules do not come into play much. The important thing is to have some rules for the time when there is a need.

Incentives

Your Co-op may also consider creating incentives for things that are important to the Co-op participants. If the Co-op wants to encourage evening sits, maybe it can increase the bonus points. The imagination can run wild when thinking of incentives using points. What if a grandma or someone special wanted to volunteer time to the Co-op? The points she earned could be distributed to all moms. This is a great way for volunteers to give a meaningful gift to all moms— especially those who need the points.

The following list of rules has been helpful to the University Place Baby-sitting Co-op. Use what fits the needs of your group and change what doesn't work. It is your Co-op; do what is necessary to make it a success.

Smart Mom's RULES

Common Sense at Work

1. You are your child's mom. It is up to you and only you, in all matters, to determine the appropriate child-care provider and environment. If a situation does not feel right, follow your instinct and good judgment. Make a promise to yourself to only rely on your own first-hand knowledge of the sitter and the child care environment.

2. A simple majority decides all votes. Amendments to Co-op guidelines require a simple majority plus one. Amendments must have a quorum of two-thirds of the group.

3. The Advisory Board consists of the Leader, past Leader, and future Leader. The Advisory Board attends home visits for applicant visit and safety review.

4. After three complaints, a participant may be dropped. The Leader must notify the participant of each complaint in reasonable time. Participants should bring complaints to the Advisory Board. Complaints must be handled promptly and privately.

5. A participant may be asked to resign due to inactivity. A participant must either request a sit or be a sitter at least once every two months. One-year-trial participants are exempt from this rule for their first year.

6. A participant must give the Co-op one month notice before resignation.

7. Participants must have a zero balance upon resignation. Positive or negative remaining points must be distributed to keep Co-op books in balance.

continued...

Common Sense at Work (continued)

8. All participants must carry standard homeowner liability insurance with a minimum coverage of $100,000. Your Co-op may be interested to invite moms who do not have homeowners insurance coverage. Be careful to discuss alternatives with professionals.

9. The sitter must have written permission and instructions to give a child medication.

10. Participants are encouraged to do sits at the requester's home if the sit goes past the kids' bedtime. Sitters are awarded a two-point bonus for doing a sit at another mom's home.

11. Each participant agrees to respect the copyrights of the Smart Mom's Baby-sitting Co-op materials. Active participants agree to re-register with Smart Mom's Baby-sitting Co-op Inc. each year. Each participant agrees to purchase their own copy of the Co-op Hand-book.

12. For rules on time keeping and points, see Chapter 13.

13. For rules on requesting a sitter, see Chapter 8.

14. For rules on being a sitter, see Chapter 9.

Meetings

What has orked best for the University Place Co-op is to hold meetings at 8:00 PM, the third Monday of the odd months. Everyone in the University place Co-op reports that the meetings are fun. Every mom reports they are always glad once they get there even if it was hard to get started out the door.

Smart Mom's RULES

Meetings That Work

The purpose of the regular meeting is to get to know each other and to coordinate calendars for future sit requests. Meetings follow a simple agenda. Business is completed quickly.

1. Attendance is required! It is important to meet the other moms who may care for your children. (And also allow for them to meet you). The Secretary records absences in the minutes. Absent participants lose two points to the Secretary.

2. The participant with the most negative points is offered the chance to host the next meeting. The host is granted one point from each participant.

3. A participant may be asked to resign after missing two consecutive meetings.

Other generally accepted rules for meetings:

4. All ideas are welcome—no put downs.

5. Only one meeting at a time—no side conversations

6. The host provides refreshments

There are six meetings per year. Regular meetings are held the third Monday of odd months at 8:00 PM (This schedule avoids most holidays.) Be prompt and bring your calendars. The 8:00 PM start allows us time to put the kids down. Meeting night is moms' night out. Be there. No excuses.

Chapter 11

Making Their Day Successful: Kids with Special Needs

A special needs child can be a wonderful addition to a Baby-sitting Co-op. Children can learn every person has challenges to overcome in life. What a great opportunity to teach lessons about tolerance, caring, and adapting to the abilities of others. These lessons are better taught now in your home than years from now somewhere else.

Parents of special needs kids can help other moms with these important lessons by lending picture books or other materials. The list of subjects is endless. There are books on all types of special needs—including divorce, adoption, mental challenges, illness, ethnicity, and many other topics. With a little planning, Co-op moms can work wonders. Think of the sits with special needs kids as an opportunity to train your child in some important lessons of life.

Most kids with special needs, or developmental disability, are not usually diagnosed during the preschool years. Since all kids are experiencing new developmental milestones in their preschool years, delays are difficult to notice. Experts advise moms to observe skill areas such as eye-hand coordination, balance, social interaction, and verbal comprehension. Parents who have concerns about their child's development might gain some insight by observing interactions with Co-op playmates at home.

"All kids have needs," says Erica Basset, mother of two. "We all would find ways to make each kid's day more successful. When you drop them off, you would talk about the nap time ritual, diet, anything. A.D.H.D. (Attention Deficit Hyperactivity Disorder) kids need to be kept busy. The sit times are short, just a couple of hours, mostly. There are lots of moms to carry the load. Challenging kids were challenging but nothing that we couldn't handle. We never had a kid that was too challenging."

Erica Bissett's family had just moved into the community. "I was just starting to find out that my son had some neurological problems. They were very subtle, not noticed in the doctor's office. The Co-op moms gave me a sense of empowerment and validation. Moms will know things about kids very well. In my work I tell moms to go with what they feel—I had to get an advanced degree to get my concerns recognized. When you have kids with problems you hesitate to join anything, but that's when you need it most."

Erica saw the Co-op as serving many needs. "Moms need to hear that problems with their kids are normal. Moms learn what's normal and what's not from each other. I see a lot of child abuse in my field of work—parents who are isolated, frustrated, with no support on how to manage a tough child. Those are variables that contribute to abuse. The success of the Co-op depended on us reaching out to others. Our stories connected; we can lean on each other."

"My son is allergic to nuts," says Mary Cline, "While everyone took care not to feed him nuts, it was at the Easter Egg Hunt that the Co-op moms automatically got candy that didn't contain nuts. I feel like these moms are really watching out for my kids. It's a good feeling."

Smart Mom's At a Glance

Special Needs Kids

- Some kids are tougher to manage than others. Moms of special needs kids need a break too—more than anyone.

- With a large number of participants, each mom can do a little and make a world of difference for a struggling family with a child with special needs.

- Accommodations for special needs kids must be discussed openly. If a situation becomes too difficult to handle, discuss that too.

- As with all kids, sits are often only a few hours. Everyone must do her part to share the load.

- It is important for participants to learn proper care instructions for special needs kids. Make an extra effort to call in a specialist to learn the details. A specialist will reinforce the commitment of participants to do their part.

- If you have any concerns, call your pediatrician. They are trained observers.

4

What Do I Do as Secretary?

Chapter 12

The Key to Being Secretary: Customer Service

The Secretary's job is the most vital part of the Co-op. You provide one-stop shopping. Moms call once for a sitter. It is up to you to make it happen. No excuses!

One person searching for sitters for everybody is better than everyone calling each other. The Secretary soon learns who needs the points and what their schedule can accommodate. This efficiency helps everybody.

Anyone can catch onto the system. Moms can turn down a sit if they have other plans. The mom requesting a sitter can turn down a sitter if she has a concern. Moms are not allowed to make a request for a special sitter. Some flexibility is given to new moms because they may not know many other moms at first.

When it comes to finding sitters, most moms will be really good at doing the sit. There is a built-in incentive—moms are eager to earn points. It will always be a fair trade, everyone is into making it work.

The Secretary position is an on-call job. Be sure that everybody can reach you. Be sure that you are quick to respond. And take care to log the sits properly.

When it is your turn to be Secretary, you will be given the Secretary's Workbook to do the job. The Secretary's Workbook has the forms used to do the day-to-day paperwork of the Co-op. It is a good idea to spend a few minutes looking over the Workbook so you can see what is needed.

Secretary Workbook Contents

The table of contents of the Secretary Workbook is listed below (see Appendix C):

Section Tab 1: Master Scheduling Worksheet
Section Tab 2: Participant Balance Sheets
Section Tab 3: End-of-Month Balancing Worksheets

Secretary's Duties

1. To serve as Secretary for one month on a rotating basis with the other moms.

2. To obtain the Secretary Workbook from the Leader on the first of the month.

3. To find sitters to fill sit requests. Sit requests are made at the meetings and by phone. For sits with less than 24 hours notice, participants must find their own sitter.

4. To record accurate and timely entry of all sits in the Scheduling Worksheet.

5. To post points to the sitter's and requester's balance sheets throughout the month.

6. *If a sitter cannot be found, the Secretary does the sit.* The most important part of the Co-op is having a sitter available every time. This rule underscores the promise your Co-op makes to every mom. In practice, the moms of the University Place Baby-sitting Co-op could not remember a time when the Secretary had to do the sit. Moms are eager to do sits to earn points. It is important to have enough moms participate to cover the sit requests.

7. To take minutes at the meetings and give them to the Leader at the end of the meeting.

8. To notify participants when their balance reaches -80 or +80 points.

9. To make sure the Workbook is organized, professional, and has adequate blank forms. The binder must be kept in good condition. Loose or torn material is not allowed. Discard old records.

Chapter 13

Secretary: How to Coordinate Sits—Do the Two-step

"The scariest time was when I was about to be Secretary. I was afraid that nobody would sit or I would mess up the points."

—Gini Walker, mother of three

Just because you feel panic, doesn't mean it's real—things normally work out. The Co-op stuff is easy but that doesn't mean your repressed math trauma won't reappear at the most inconvenient time. If you are experiencing anxiety, think of it as a fitting punishment for not paying attention when you were in math class. Let the stress run its course. It's too late. No use trying to overcome it now. Just try to limit the strange behavior—the goal is to spare the kids.

No matter what burden you carry from childhood, the fact is the job has to be done. Do your best to keep track of points and return calls promptly for quick customer service. Enough said.

When You Get a Call for a Sit

Record the sit request in the Master Scheduling Worksheet immediately. (See your Secretary Workbook) Check to see if the participant balance sheets are arranged in order with those with the most debt on top. When you search for a sitter, call those with the most point

75

debt first. When you find a sitter, record the name and phone number in the Master Scheduling Worksheet and then call the requester and tell her the sitter's name.

Two-Step Process

1 Record the sit on the Master Scheduling Worksheet (names, hours, points, etc.). The Master Scheduling Worksheet must record information on all point transactions (including bonus and penalty points). When the sit is complete the sitter will call you with her hours. Look up the point amount from the point chart in Chapter 17 and enter the points in the Scheduling Worksheet.

2 Record a positive (+) point amount on the sitter's balance sheet and a negative (-) point amount on the requester's balance sheet. After you do this, be sure to put a check mark in the Master Scheduling Worksheet to show the sit has been posted.

Points do not just come out of thin air. And points do not vanish. To keep Co-op records accurate, points are always transferred from one person to another. This is done by entering positive points for the sitter and negative points for the requester. For every sit, the positive points offset the negative points. If you add up all negative points for the whole Co-op, and then do the same for all positive points, the two totals should always be the same (except for the + or - sign). The same is true for the total of the points on the Master Scheduling Worksheet.

Participants earn points from sitting. There are other ways to earn points. Be sure to record the bonus and penalty points listed below on the Scheduling Worksheet in the Secretary Workbook. Then, as with a sit, post the points to the participant balance sheets.

Smart Mom's RULES

Time-Keeping and Points

1. Time starts at the time scheduled rather than the time of arrival of the requester.

2. Time is counted to the next full quarter-hour.

3. The number of hours earned should be agreed upon by the parties at the end of the sit.

4. If the requester returns one hour late, the sitter can report to the Secretary time and one half for time beyond the scheduled return.

5. Actual sit hours and the number of kids are reported to the Secretary within one week of the sit. Points are figured from the Secretary's point chart. Four points are granted for a one-hour sit for one child. The sitter earns an additional two points per hour for each additional child.

Bonus and Penalty Points

1. Credit yourself (Secretary) with two points from each participant at the end of your term.

2. Credit the hostess of a meeting with one point from each participant.

3. Credit the Leader with four-points from each participant *at the end of the Leader's six-month rotation.*

4. Credit the Secretary two points from participants who missed meetings.

continued...

Bonus and Penalty Points *(continued)*

5. Transfer an additional two points for evening sits done at the requester's home.

6. Penalize the sitter two points for failing to report sit hours within one week after the sit. Transfer the two-points to the Secretary.

7. Penalize the sitter for defaulting on a sit. Transfer the estimated points of the intended sit from the defaulting sitter to the requester.

How to Record Bonus and Penalty Points

The best thing to do is to make things as simple as possible. Assume your Co-op has a total of 10 moms. Lets also say that the Leader's term is up and the rules say that each mom (nine other moms) must transfer four points to the Leader.

It is best to count all 10 moms (including the Leader) when figuring bonus points. If you count just the "nine other moms" things get a little bit complicated. To make things simple, count *all* the moms in the Co-op, if the bonus paid to the Leader is four points from each mom, then record 40 points earned on the Master Scheduling Sheet as a "bonus earned from all moms." (40 points = 4 pts each X 10 moms)

Next, be sure to make an entry for *everyone* in their Participant Balance Sheet for -4 points *paid*. The Leader will have two entries on her Balance sheet. +40 bonus *earned* and a -4 bonus *paid*.

In this example it may seem odd to make two entries for the leader. Even so, this trick is useful when you are doing a bonus for more than one person, Secretary, Hostess, and Leader. The above method allows us to make the general rule that each *bonus paid* entry is the same for all moms—even if you are the Secretary, Leader, or Hostess.

For example, assume you need to pay out bonuses to the Secretary (two points), the Hostess of a meeting (one point), and the Leader (four points). Using the above method, it is easy to combine these three bonuses into one entry in each Participant Balance Sheet: "Bonuses paid: -7 points". It is easier to make 10 combined entries that are exactly the same for everyone, than it is to make three separate entries for every mom.

- When figuring the total *bonus* count *every mom in the Co-op* including the person who will get the bonus.

  Total Bonus = Bonus point allowed X number of all moms

- When making entries on the Participant Balance Sheets for the *bonus paid*, make an entry in the Balance Sheet of *every mom in the Co-op*, including the person(s) who got the bonus.

- The Secretary's balance sheet will show an entry of "seven points paid." It will also show a bonus of two points from 10 moms: "20 point bonus."

- The Leader Balance Sheetwill show an entry of "seven points paid." It will also show a bonus of four points from ten moms: "40 point bonus."

How to Do End-of-Month Check
Avoid frustration. At the end of your term complete the End-of-Month Worksheet found in the Secretary Workbook.

What to Do When a Participant Resigns

When a participant resigns, their balance sheet is marked *inactive* and filed away. Once a balance sheet is marked inactive it is <u>not</u> part of the end-of-month balance process. Every sit has a negative entry on one balance sheet and a positive entry on someone else's balance sheet. So if one balance sheet is filed away with points on it, the Co-op books will not balance at the end of the month.

The easiest way to keep the books in balance is to ask the mom who is resigning to do sits (or have a sitter) so that her balance is exactly zero when she leaves. If this is not possible, distribute her remaining point balance equally to all participants.

Smart Mom's RULES

End-of-Month Checks and Balances

1. Check to see that all sits are recorded on the Master Scheduling Worksheet.

2. Check that each record (i.e. sit) in the Scheduling Worksheet has a corresponding entry in the sitter and requester balance sheets.

3. Check to see that bonus points have been posted as required.

4. Complete the End-of-month Worksheet.

5. Draw a line under the last sit you entered in the Scheduling Worksheet during your term and pass on the Workbook. You are done!

Favorite Sitter Requests

Moms often have favorite sitters. Moms may live close to another mom, the moms may have kids that match up, they may be close friends. Whatever the reason, moms will have a tendency to have someone in mind when they want a sitter. Do not grant special requests.

What could happen if participants were allowed to pick their sitter every time? Most moms of the University Place Baby-sitting Co-op said it would spell disaster. The person with the most negative points must have the opportunity to earn points and get out of the hole. When moms use only their favorite sitter, it makes it hard for new participants to break into the Co-op. This defeats the purpose of the Co-op.

The Co-op is a service. Favorite sit requests can make life easier on the participants. As Secretary, it is your job to encourage participants to use the sitter who has the most negative points. On the other hand, reasonable flexibility is always helpful—especially for new moms who may not know everyone.

Sitter Point Earnings Chart

Points are figured from the Secretary's point chart. Four points are granted for a one-hour sit for one child. The sitter earns an additional two points per hour for each additional child.

Actual Hours	One Child	Two Children	Three Children	Four Children
1.00	4	6	8	10
1.25	5	8	10	13
1.50	6	9	12	15
1.75	7	11	14	18
2.00	8	12	16	20
2.25	9	14	18	23
2.50	10	15	20	25
2.75	11	17	22	28
3.00	12	18	24	30
3.25	13	20	26	33
3.50	14	21	28	35
3.75	15	23	30	38
4.00	16	24	32	40
4.25	17	26	34	43
4.50	18	27	36	45
4.75	19	29	38	48
5.00	20	30	40	50
5.25	21	32	42	53
5.50	22	33	44	55
5.75	23	35	46	58
6.00	24	36	48	60
6.25	25	38	50	63
6.50	26	39	52	65
6.75	27	41	54	68
7.00	28	42	56	70
7.25	29	44	58	73
7.50	30	45	60	75
7.75	31	47	62	78
8.00	32	48	64	80

5

What Do I Do as Leader?

Chapter 14

The Key to Being Leader: See the Big Picture

Moms can mobilize with military precision. Baby showers, get-well cards, fund raising, you name it. There is nothing stopping moms on a mission! So what is the mission?

When you become the Co-op Leader, you are joining many others who have been the caretaker of the Co-op for a time and have passed it on to new moms. The main function of the Leader is to look ahead and keep things on track. See the big picture.

Your term is six months. You are not alone. The past Leader and the future Leader will be there for you when you need them. Whenever you need to talk or work things out, give them a call. They are a great resource.

> The purpose of the Co-op is to help mothers of preschoolers have some time out so moms can better care for them-selves, their families, and each other.

The Leader's role is to help moms cus-tomize Co-op rules to meet the groups' needs, expectations, and values. Discuss the issues and vote if necessary. But be careful. Some changes may cause more trouble than they're worth. Keep changes simple so they can be passed to the next generation of moms with the Workbooks to survive the years.

Six secretaries will serve during your term. It is your job to see that the Secretary Workbook is transferred to the next Secretary properly. Make sure each Secretary understands her job and is responsive to the needs of the participants. When you transfer the Workbook from one Secretary to another, check to see that the points balance. When you deliver the Workbook to the next Secretary, spend some time and review how things work.

The sign of a healthy Co-op is 15 active participants. With 15 moms, you will seldom get caught without a sitter. If group numbers are down, it is up to the Leader to sign up new participants. If participants seem inactive, give them a call. Plan ahead. Decide how many new participants you want to join during your term. Then, get started early so you have plenty of time to achieve your goals.

Moms may not like the thought of having a negative point balance. Remind participants that if everybody stayed at zero they would never have time out. It is a good thing to use the Co-op. If necessary, the Leader can make up incentives and friendly penalties to promote

Smart Mom's T I P S

Avoid Disaster

One year, the University Place Baby-sitting Co-op discovered that half the moms (and their kids) were about to resign out of the Co-op because the kids were all school-age. The Co-op had to scramble to recruit new moms to take their place to make sure the Co-op was strong enough to continue.

activity. "Use eight points in the next month or forfeit eight points to the mom who wins the next door prize." It's your Co-op. Have fun with it.

Leader's Duties

Term: Serve for six months on a rotating basis. (The term runs January through June, and July through December.) *The Leader who serves during the Fall term is responsible for the annual September registration and fee collection.*

Lead Meetings: Meetings are held the third Monday of odd months at 8:00 PM.

All meeting times and dates will present scheduling conflicts. It is recommended that the Co-op adopt this meeting time unless there is a good reason to consider a change. Meetings in odd months avoid most holidays. Monday meetings avoid conflicts with other typical weekly meetings. The 8:00 PM start time allows participants to put the kids to bed before the meeting.

Keep Minutes: Mail minutes to all participants within one week after the meeting. It is the Secretary's job to take minutes.

Assist Secretary: Review the Secretary's Workbook at the end of each month and deliver it to the next Secretary on the rotation list. (It is the Secretary's job to balance the points using the End-of-Month Worksheet before returning the Secretary's Workbook to the Leader.)

New Participants: Coordinate recruitment and registration of new participants.

87

Authorization for Medical Treatment Forms: Continue to make sure that each mom has a form from all other moms.

Home Visits: Arrange the home visit for each potential new participant. See the step-by step instructions in Chapter 16.

Treasury: Record income and expenses. Retain receipts of purchases. Participant Directory—Make sure the Participant Directory in the Leader Workbook is updated with the names of new participants. Look to the check boxes next to each name in the Participant Directory to verify that registration, proof of insurance, and fees have been received. Collect outstanding items before you pass on the Workbook to the next Leader.

Reward: The Leader gets four points at the end of her six-month term from each participant if safety is discussed at every meeting.

Workbooks: Make sure Workbooks are organized, complete, and have adequate blank forms. Safeguard original forms.

Smart Mom's TIPS

Meetings That Work

- Do not meet too frequently. The suggested schedule of one meeting every two months is about right for moms to get to know each other and do business. Start the meeting promptly and do business first, then visit.

- Studies show that those who speak up early in a meeting are more likely to participate throughout the meeting. Get moms to talk early and often.

- Follow the sample agenda provided in the Leader Workbook.

- The Leader, Secretary, and host should call to remind participants of the time and place. Think of an interesting teaser that you can announce to get people's attention and attendance.

- Make the meeting fun. Have a small door prize or gag-gift drawing at the end.

- Food!

Sample Meeting Minutes

University Place Baby-sitting Co-op
May 18, 1999
At the home of Judy Parker

Present: Laura, Terri, Patty, Judy, Neva, and Vicki Strong (New).

Next Hostess and Meeting Date: July 20th at 8pm at Patty's house 8498 South 18th Street. (565-4889)

Treasury Report: Current balance of $75.29. Fees paid by Neva. Fees owed by Lori and Vicki. * We need copies of medical release forms from Sue Shoemaker, Leisha Topel, Vicki Strong, and Pam Sandersen.

Secretary Rotation:
June - Sue Shoemaker	565-5555
July - Pam Sandersen	565-8888
August - Neva Toppen	564-3333

Leader Rotation:
July - December:	Leisha Topel	564-1111
December - June:	Jean Cuttingham	571-4444

Safety: We talked about doing another CPR class this fall.

New Business: We welcomed a new Co-op member, Vicki Strong! We talked about some play dates for the summer. We will meet at a park once a month during the summer and let the kids play and we can visit! Play dates are as follows: Thursday, June 25, Titlow big toy; Thursday, July 16, Chambers Elementary; Thursday, August 13, Fircrest tot lot. All play dates will start at 10:30; bring a lunch if you want!

Old Business: The Myers are still working on a book about the Co-op. They would like input to put in the book so please take a few minutes to fill out the enclosed questionnaire and drop it in the mail.

Leader Workbook Contents

Baby-sitting Co-op Boundary Certificate
Section 1:   Participant Directory
Section 2:   September Registration and Fee Collection
Section 3:   Authorization for Medical Treatment
Section 4:   Re-usable Agenda
Section 5:   Leader and Secretary Rotation Lists
Section 6:   Baby-sitting Co-op Interest List (sign-up sheet)
              Baby-sitting Co-op Pamphlet (front and back)
Section 7:   Treasury Records
              Pencil pouch to hold dues money
Section 8:   Heartfelt good-byes: Resignation cards
Appendix A (Copies of original forms):
              Participant Directory
              September Registration and Fee Collection
              Authorization for Medical Treatment
              Safety Visit Checklist
              Treasury Record
              End-of-Month Worksheet
              Reusable Agenda   See Appendix C
              Leader Rotation List   for sample
              Secretary Rotation List   forms.
              Master Scheduling Worksheet
              Baby-sitting Co-op Interest List (sign-up sheet)
              Bulletin Board Poster
              Baby-sitting Co-op Pamphlet (front and back)
              Smart Mom's Co. Order Form

Chapter 15

Tips to Find Interested Moms: Get the Word Out

The best way to recruit new moms is by word-of-mouth. That means words coming forth, out of your mouth, when others are present to hear them. No mumbling!

You will be surprised at the number of moms who cross your path. Just tell them about the Co-op. Before long you will have a waiting list of moms who want to join.

First things first. Talk with all co-op moms. Discuss how they want to sign on new participants. It is important that everyone is comfortable with how an interested mom is granted the invitation to join.

It is vital to keep the group close and personal so that trusting relationships develop. Participants must be able to trust each other to care for their children. And moms must know that each commitment for baby-sitting is reliable. Develop your recruitment plan with this in mind.

If the Co-op is nearly full, or if there is concern a prospective participant is outside the Co-op boundary, no big deal—just help them form another Co-op! Help them get started! Sponsor them! Consider buying a Smart Mom's Baby-sitting Co-op Handbook as a gift.

Interest List or Waiting list?

The posting of an interest list is another way to find potential participants. But be careful where you choose to post it. It is not a good
practice to extend invitations to the general public to join the Co-op.
If you decide to post a list for interested moms, here's how:

First buy a poster board in your favorite color. Second, go to the
Leader Workbook and make a copy of the "Interest List Sign up
Sheet" in your next favorite color. Last of all, make a copy of the
three-fold "Baby-sitting Co-op Pamphlet" in your third favorite color.

Tape the Interest List Sign-up Sheet to the poster board. Place the
pamphlets in a homemade pamphlet-holder stapled vigorously to the
poster board. Check to make sure that your three favorite colors
don't frighten people away.

Check the interest list each week. If you return and find eight or
more signed up in the first week, this is a good indication that you
should consider sponsoring another Co-op.

Gather the names and phone numbers. Assign one mom to each name
on the interest list and have them call the new moms to answer questions. Then plan a way for participants to meet applicants. A play-date
at a park worked well for the University Place Co-op—moms can watch
their kids and visit at the same time.

See the Leaders's Workbook for original copies of posters and pamphlets.

Chapter 16

A Special Way To Enroll a New Mom: The Home Visit

It is important the Co-op has enough participants so someone is always available to sit when needed. But it is also important to make sure that those invited to join are reliable and trustworthy.

Smart Mom's TIPS

How The University Place Co-op Enrolls a New Mom

- The moms of the University Place Co-op check to see if the prospective mom lives within a reasonable driving distance to be a sitter.

- Next, each prospective mom must be sponsored by a Co-op mom that knows her well and is willing to make the recommendation to the Co-op.

- Then three Co-op moms do a home-visit to get to know the mom and to discuss safety. The new mom will know at least four Co-op moms—this will help break the ice when she attends her first meeting.

Unless your Co-op modifies the process, the invitation to join is extended only upon a unanimous vote of the three moms that show up for the home visit (Usually the past, current and future Co-op Leaders). Some Co-ops have a practice of voting on the applicant during the home visit so they can complete the sign up at the same time. Other Co-ops prefer to delay the vote for discussions with the whole group. Either way is okay--just plan ahead.

In any case, it is best to do your homework before the home visit. The Leader should delay the home visit until the recommendation from the sponsoring mom is thorough and reliable. You should be 95% sure of the applicant before the home visit. The home visit should be a confirmation of what you already know as well as a time to focus on safety.

It is easy to move ahead and vote during the home visit when everyone is confident of the applicant. It is very difficult to be diplomatic and delay the process if someone has a concern. Have a prearranged signal that everyone knows so that each of you can delay the vote if a concern arises during the home visit. Otherwise, it is convenient for everyone to do the paperwork at the end of the home visit.

During the home visit read over the Co-op rules. Do the home safety check. Then have the new mom turn to the back of her Co-op Handbook to complete the registration forms.

After the invitation is extended to the new mom, make a special effort to contact her personally to invite her to the first few meetings.

New participants are usually close friends with only one or two other moms in the Co-op when they join. Offer a few suggestions and some encouraging words. It takes time to get to know other moms well enough to ask them to watch your kids. Help new moms ease into the Co-op at their own pace.

Smart Mom's RULES

Before the Home Visit

1. Verify that a sponsoring mom is *very* familiar with the new mom and her home environment, and that she lives within the Co-op boundaries. The sponsor's recommendation is the most important step of all.

2. Use the money in the Co-op treasury to buy a copy of the Co-op Handbook in advance so that you will have a copy that you can leave with the new mom. Every participant must own a Co-op Handbook. The new mom can repay the treasury when she starts.

3. Call the new mom and introduce yourself. Explain the process for sign up. Schedule the home visit with the past and future Leaders. Be sure to tell the applicant that you will collect a participant fee plus the cost of the Smart Mom's Baby-sitting Co-op Handbook.

4. Explain that her participation in the Co-op will be registered with Smart Mom's Co. The registration form can be found in the back of her Co-op Handbook. (It is the Leader's job to send the registrations to the address listed for Smart Mom's Co.)

5. Ask the applicant to call her insurance agent to obtain proof of homeowners insurance with a minimum liability of $100,000. (The insurance company might be able to send it directly to the Leader's address.)

6. It is best to drop off a copy of the Co-op Handbook before the site visit.

continued...

Smart Mom's Rules *(continued)*

During the Home Visit

1. Do a safety check—find the check list in the Leader Workbook.

2. Collect your local Co-op participation fee ($6 to $10 suggested) plus the cost of the Co-op Handbook. (Be sure to collect enough to stock a few Co-op Handbooks.)

3. Collect the signed registration forms from the back of the new mom's Co-op Handbook.

4. Collect proof of homeowner liability insurance.

5. Collect the Authorization for Medical Treatment.

6. Bring the Leader Workbook for reference.

7. Lend the applicant a Smart Mom's Baby-sitting Co-op Handbook.

After the Home Visit

1. New moms are the featured guests at meetings—be sure the new moms attend their first meeting.

2. Record the new name in the Participant Directory in the Leader Workbook. Next to the name, put a date in the box for receipt of the participation fee, registration, and proof of insurance, as appropriate.

3. Call the Secretary to start a Balance Sheet for the new participant.

4. Send a copy of the registration to Smart Mom's Co., c/o Tukwila Book Publishers Inc., 8408 S. 18th Street, W., Tacoma, WA 98465.

Chapter 17

The September Meeting:
Annual Registration and Fees

> The September registration is a renewal of the registration
> of existing participants. To register a new participant see
> Chapter 16 and use the Registration form in the back of their
> Co-op Handbook.

The purpose of the September Meeting is to update records of
participation, and to follow a special September meeting agenda that
focuses on safety and planning. The September registration process
also provides a means for the Leader to verify that each participant's
homeowner's insurance is current.

What to Do as Leader

1 Go to the section *September Registration* in the Leader Work
book. Send a copy of the Registration form to all participants.
Be sure the Co-op ID number is legible on the original so it will copy
well on every registration form.

2 At the September meeting, include the discussion questions
found on the Special September Meeting Agenda located on
page 102.

3 It is the Leader's job to collect from each participant, the signed forms, fees, etc. (These things are itemized on the September Registration form you send to each participant).

4 When a participant gives you their completed registration materials, be sure to date, in the appropriate box by the names in the Participant Directory, receipt of 1) the local participation fees, 2) The Smart Mom's Co. fee, and 3) proof of homeowner's insurance.

5 Total the amount of the fees collected from all participants and enter the total as a single deposit in the Treasury section in the Leader Workbook. Place the money in the pencil pouch in the Leader Workbook. (Receipt of fees and deposits are recorded by placing a date in the Participant Directory next to each participant's name). Do not record each payment check in the Treasury record—just the total deposit.

6 Send a copy of the registration renewal forms and checks to:

Smart Mom's Co.
c/o Tukwila Book Publishers Inc.
8408 South 18th Street, W.
Tacoma, WA 98465

7 Place the original copies of the Registration Form and the Proof of Insurance letters in the Leader Workbook. Find and discard records from last year.

How Do I Explain the Fees?

The local participant fee is for get-well cards, cookies, shower gifts, cookies, supplies and stamps, cookies, and other important things like cookies! This fee amount is set by participants each year to cover costs.

The Smart Mom's Co. registration fee is also important (Almost as important as cookies). This fee is less than the cost of two postage stamps a month. Compared to the advantages of belonging to a Co-op, most moms will agree the registration fee equal to fifty cents a month is a small amount.

What Does Our Co-op Get for Registration with Smart Mom's Co.?

Your Baby-sitting Co-op is much more than a book. Your Baby-sitting Co-op is about people. Your Co-op may continue to exist for decades. The materials and needs of your Co-op will change from time to time. There is merit to the idea of providing a way for one Co-op group to learn from the experiences of other Co-op groups.

It is difficult to anticipate what needs may arise and what other services might prove useful in the future. Even so, plans must be made to provide some degree of support service—that is what the fee is for.

The registration fee is important to the planning, development, and presentation of quality Web/newsletter content for on-going support of Baby-sitting Co-ops everywhere.

All Co-ops will utilize the free download of Co-op forms at one time or another—especially when the original forms are accidentally used-up. Also, innovations and revisions to Co-op forms may one-day provide additional benefits to you and your Co-op.

While some individuals may not be interested in Web page material, the information is vital to many new and growing Co-op groups. Most would agree it is necessary for all to share in the support of such service. Otherwise, resources may not be adequate to keep it going.

All things considered, the benefit of participating in a Co-op must surely outweigh the necessary fees to provide basic means of communication and support of new and growing Baby-sitting Co-ops.

Special September Meeting Agenda

1. What kinds of accidents have happened to our own kids?

2. How can we prevent accidents in our homes?

3. The role of the Co-op is to facilitate baby-sitting among friends, not certify character of participants. What does this mean?

4. Why is it important to let moms learn about other moms from first-hand experience and not from participant advice when using a sitter?

5. How is our Co-op going to evaluate moms who want to participate?

6. House Keeping—Does everyone have the medical authorizations in order? Do we have any special needs kids that need special care or have a medical condition we should learn more about?

7. What else should we discuss? Are we forgetting anything?

8. What about planning some play dates at a park so we can get together?

Appendix A

Practice Before You Play: Follow the Flow Charts

Even though the idea of a Co-op is not too complex, it pays to make sure everyone understands how it works. It is good to role-play. Work your way through the flow charts. Be sure to review how the Secretary does her job to find a sitter and record points. The Secretary and Leader Workbooks will be needed to get the most from these flow charts.

How Things Work— It's Simple!

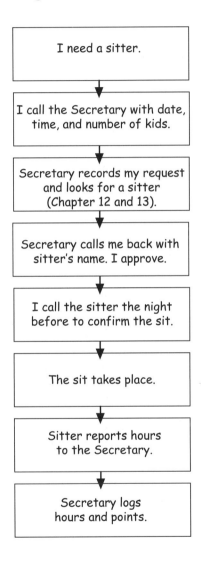

I need a sitter.

⬇

I call the Secretary with date, time, and number of kids.

⬇

Secretary records my request and looks for a sitter (Chapter 12 and 13).

⬇

Secretary calls me back with sitter's name. I approve.

⬇

I call the sitter the night before to confirm the sit.

⬇

The sit takes place.

⬇

Sitter reports hours to the Secretary.

⬇

Secretary logs hours and points.

How to Enroll a New Mom
(See Chapter 16)

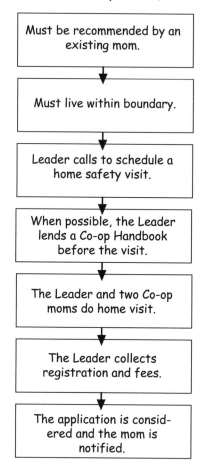

Must be recommended by an existing mom.

Must live within boundary.

Leader calls to schedule a home safety visit.

When possible, the Leader lends a Co-op Handbook before the visit.

The Leader and two Co-op moms do home visit.

The Leader collects registration and fees.

The application is considered and the mom is notified.

How to Start a New Baby-sitting Co-op

(See Chapters 5
and 6)

Order four Co-op Handbooks,
and the Leader and Secretary
Workbooks.

Invite three friends over
for one hour.

Determine Co-op boundaries
to minimize driving time.

Register yourself and three
friends.

Select the first Leader and
first Secretary.

Start a "Participant Balance
Sheet" for each mom.

Complete the discussion
checklist (Chapter 5).

Identify other moms to
invite—lend a Co-op Hand-
book for their review.

Hold a meeting every two
months to introduce new
moms.

How the Secretary Balances
End-of-Month Points
(See Chapter 13)

Add up all positive points awarded this month.

Add up all negative points awarded this month.

Add up all the points recorded in the Scheduling Worksheet this month.

Are these three totals equal numbers (except for the + or - sign)?

Appendix B

Terms of Baby-sitting Co-op Participation

I understand that my local Baby-sitting Co-op is not incorporated and does not have legal status as an organization. Although the Co-op materials use terms like *application* and *participation*, I understand that these terms are used to communicate ideas. The participants are not members of an organization. I agree to practice the guidelines suggested in the Smart Mom's Baby-sitting Co-op materials and other rules recognized by other participants. In this way, participation in this Baby-sitting Co-op is similar to participating in other recurring group activity such as playing volleyball with friends.

I understand that a copy of my registration will be sent to Tukwila Book Publishers Inc. as a record of my participation in my local Co-op. I understand that I am not joining a national organization or national association. Although Tukwila Book Publishers Inc. may provide a useful service like a newsletter or web site, this is done on a voluntary basis. Such service will be intermittent and may be subject to errors and omissions.

I understand the forms and materials contained in the Smart Mom's Baby-sitting Co-op Handbook and associated workbooks, will be treated like any other copyrighted material. I understand that I may copy this material while I am a registered participant of this local Co-op. My use of materials does not include copying material for the purpose of starting another Baby-sitting Co-op or making a copy of the Smart Mom's Baby-sitting Co-op Handbook for another participant.

I understand that the function of the local Co-op is to *facilitate* the exchange of baby-sitting among my friends. While Co-op participants may review an applicant and her home prior to granting an invitation to participate, I agree that I will only rely on my first-hand knowledge when considering using a sitter. I will not rely on Co-op participants, the Leader, the Secretary, the author, or the publisher when determining the proper baby-sitter and care environment for my children.

I hereby agree the duty, responsibility, and liability that is inherent with baby-sitting (either as the sitter, as the requester, or as the child) shall remain as it would be if the parties were not part of any Baby-sitting Co-op. I agree to leave intact the normal remedies and cause-of-action available to these parties in the event of an accident or worse.

I agree to indemnify and hold harmless all other third parties who have facili-tated the baby-sitting arrangement(s) in question. I agree to hold harmless those participants who arrange baby-sitting or do other Co-op activity. I agree the same shall not extend to a Co-op participant while acting as my sitter (or if I am the sitter, the requester).

Disclaimer

The purpose of this book is to inspire, educate, entertain, and to provide ele-ments of organization that may help facilitate baby-sitting exchanges. You are urged to read all other available material, learn as much as possible about child safety, parenting, and Baby-sitting Co-ops and adapt the information you learn to your individual needs. This book should be used only as a general guide and contains information current only to the date of printing.

This book and associated workbooks are made available with the understanding that the publisher, author, and Tukwila Book Publishers Inc. are not providing legal or other professional services. The author, publisher, and Smart Mom's Inc. shall have neither liability nor responsibility to any person or entity with respect to loss, damage, or injury caused, or alleged to be caused, directly or indirectly by the information contained in this book or associated workbook materials.

If you do not wish to be bound by the above, you may return this book to the publisher for a refund.

Appendix C

Sample forms from the Leader and Secretary Workbooks

Participant Directory

(Keep all history of past participants. Enter date (mo/yr) in the appropriate boxes.)

Join Date: _____   Retire Date: _____

Name: _____   Participant Fee: | | | | | |
Phone: _____   Smart Mom's Fee: | | | | | |
                                  Proof of Insurance: | | | | | |

Join Date: _____   Retire Date: _____

Name: _____   Participant Fee: | | | | | |
Phone: _____   Smart Mom's Fee: | | | | | |
                                  Proof of Insurance: | | | | | |

Join Date: _____   Retire Date: _____

Name: _____   Participant Fee: | | | | | |
Phone: _____   Smart Mom's Fee: | | | | | |
                                  Proof of Insurance: | | | | | |

Join Date: _____   Retire Date: _____

Name: _____   Participant Fee: | | | | | |
Phone: _____   Smart Mom's Fee: | | | | | |
                                  Proof of Insurance: | | | | | |

Join Date: _____   Retire Date: _____

Name: _____   Participant Fee: | | | | | |
Phone: _____   Smart Mom's Fee: | | | | | |
                                  Proof of Insurance: | | | | | |

Join Date: _____   Retire Date: _____

Name: _____   Participant Fee: | | | | | |
Phone: _____   Smart Mom's Fee: | | | | | |
                                  Proof of Insurance: | | | | | |

Join Date: _____   Retire Date: _____

Name: _____   Participant Fee: | | | | | |
Phone: _____   Smart Mom's Fee: | | | | | |
                                  Proof of Insurance: | | | | | |

Participant Balance Sheet

Participant: _____ Phone: _____

Spouse: _____ Number of Children: _____

Schedule Restrictions: _____

Evenings and Weekends: (yes/no) _____

Date	I Sat For:	(+) Points	Sat For Me:	(-) Points	Balance

Master Scheduling Worksheet

Date	The Sit is For:	# Kids	Date & Time	Sit Done By:	Hours	Points	✓ Posted

End-of-Month Worksheet

A	B	C	D	E	F	
Name/Date	Total Points You Recorded from Master Log	Total (+) Points You Transferred to Sitters	Total (-) Points You Transferred From Requesters	Running Total Positive Point Balances Combined	Running Total Negative Point Balances Combined	Comments

1) Columns B, C and D must all be equal.
2) Columns E and F must be equal.
3) Column B shows sit activity during your term. A healthy co-op will have at least half of all participants use the co-op for two hours. If Column B is consistently less than 60, talk to the Leader about recruiting more moms to call for more sits.

Leader Rotation List: Who's Next?

(Usually appointed in order of start date)

Jan-June   _____Phone_____

July-Dec   _____Phone_____

Jan-June   _____Phone_____

July-Dec   _____Phone_____

Jan-June   _____Phone_____

July-Dec   _____Phone_____

Jan-June   _____Phone_____

July-Dec   _____Phone_____

Jan-June   _____Phone_____

July-Dec   _____Phone_____

Secretary Rotation: Who's Next?

(Usually appointed in order of start date)

September _____Phone_____

October _____Phone_____

November _____Phone_____

December _____Phone_____

January _____Phone_____

February _____Phone_____

March _____Phone_____

April _____Phone_____

May _____Phone_____

June _____Phone_____

July _____Phone_____

August _____Phone_____

About the Author

Gary Myers is the father of Kelly, Robin, and Logan and lives in Tacoma Washington with his lovely wife Patty.

Mr. Myers earned a Masters of Science and has studied business process modeling at the University of Washington. He enjoys the challenge of re-engineering business activities into their simplest and most efficient form. This book is the result of doing this with the University Place Baby-sitting Co-op.

Gary Myers looks for concepts having wide-spread application. He then studies the activity and creates a step-by-step business solution with everything needed for success.

Please write him if you have ideas that might fit his format.

Smart Mom's Co.
c/o Tukwila Book Publishers Inc.
8408 S. 18th Street, W.
Tacoma, WA 98465

Call 1-888-974-2667 for our web site address and other information about how to order Smart Mom's Baby-sitting Co-op Handbook and Workbooks.

Smart Mom's Inc.
Registration of Participation
(Use this form only when registering for the first time)

Unlike most how–to books, the Smart Mom's Baby-sitting Co-op Handbook would not be complete without the stuff necessary to meet basic organizational needs—including registration of participants. Although a registration process may seem to be a bit formal for a small group of friends who might be new to the idea behind a Baby-sitting Co-op, the need for this formality is well founded. Your Co-op may exist for years. It is best to equip your Co-op with basic organizational stuff needed for continued success. Please see Chapter 17 for more information.

The Co-op Leader will need the following in order for you to participate:

- This signed registration form and agreement to the terms of participation (see Appendix B).

- A check for your local participation fee—usually ($6–$10) per year plus the cost of the Co-op Handbook .

- Proof of homeowner's liability insurance having $100,000 minimum. (Available from your insurance agent)

Your local participation fee is for get-well cards, cookies, shower gifts, cookies, supplies and stamps, cookies, and other important things like cookies. In addition, a Smart Mom's Co. registration is also important. Almost as important as cookies. Participants must re-register their participation with Smart Mom's Co. each year during September. This fee ($6 per year) is not required now. See Chapter 17).

Leader's job: Forward a copy of this registration to the Smart Mom's Co., c/o Tukwila Book Publishers as record of participation—no fee is necessary until September.

Agreement

I have read the terms of participation and the disclaimer in Appendix B of this Baby-sitting Co-op Handbook and hereby acknowledge the disclaimer and agree to the rules and terms of participation.

Signature_____ Date_____ Print Name_____

Address: _____ State: _____ Zip: _____ Phone:_____

Co-op ID Number (from Leader Workbook): [   ]

This information will not be sold or provided to non-participants. Your address may be used to mail newsletter information. Please check to see that the Co-op ID number is on this form.

Authorization for Medical Treatment

Parents: _____ Date: _____

Phone: _____ _____ _____ _____

Address: _____

Children: _____ _____ _____ _____

Birth-date: _____ _____ _____ _____

Conditions, Allergies etc.: _____

Emergency Contacts: _____

Pediatrician: _____Phone: _____

Insurance: _____Phone: _____

We authorize _____ to give consent to surgical or medical treatment by a licensed physician or hospital for our children listed above when such treatment is deemed necessary by a physician and neither parent can be reached within a reasonable amount of time.

Such consent may include anesthetics, medical treatment, tests, X-rays, pharmaceutical drugs, and surgery. It is understood that this authorization is given in advance of specific diagnosis or hospital care and must be used only for emergency treatment.

_____   _____
        Parent Signature   Parent signature

(At the first meeting, new participants are to provide a copy of this completed form to each Co-op mom and one copy for the Leader Workbook.)

Smart Mom's Co. Order Form

Smart Mom's Baby-sitting Co-op Handbook and Workbooks

This is the best thing ever invented for moms to help moms! Your friends will thank you! When you want a sitter, make one call to the Secretary and expect it to happen every time! Simple to start. Easy to run. Do your turn. Then you are done! The Co-op is designed to thrive without you!

Each participant must have their own Co-op Handbook. Each baby-sitting Co-op must have the Leader Workbook and the Secretary Workbook. Workbooks can be purchased from the publisher or downloaded from our web-site for free. It takes four moms to start a Co-op—each will need a Handbook.

Smart Mom's Baby-sitting Co-op Handbook: Explains the rules and how to start a Baby-sitting Co-op. (If you are starting a new Co-op, you will also need the Workbooks for Leader and Secretary.)

Sold individually	$14.95 each plus shipping
Package of (4)*	$50 plus shipping
Package of (10)*	$100 plus shipping

Secretary Workbook and the Leader Workbook: These workbooks have all the paperwork and forms needed for day-to-day operation of your Baby-sitting Co-op. When you are the Secretary or Leader, you will have the Workbook to go with the job. (Your Co-op Handbook tells you how to use the Workbooks.)

Leader and Secretary Workbooks sold together—three hole punched for your notebooks for $14.95 each. Or down load these free from our web site.

Call 1–888–974–2667 for the web site address and any other information on how to order Smart Mom's Baby–sitting Co–op Handbooks.

*If you are ordering a package of books, a set of workbooks can be substituted in place of one co–op handbook in the package upon request.
Prices are current only to the date of publication.

Notes

Notes